A
Delicate
Strength:

A Delicate Strength:

GOD'S DESIGN OF A WOMAN

Peggi Klubnik

XULON PRESS

Xulon Press
555 Winderley Pl, Suite 225
Maitland, FL 32751
407.339.4217
www.xulonpress.com

Paperback ISBN-13: 978-1-66289-303-2
eBook ISBN-13: 978-1-66289-304-9

Dedication

This book is dedicated to my husband, Jim, who loved me dearly and always provided support of my endeavors in teaching, writing and painting. He loved to laugh. He loved his family. But more than that he loved the Lord. He encouraged me to study the Bible and loved teaching the Bible and sharing the gospel. He was a great father to our two sons, Jon and Tod, and enjoyed spending time with them and their families.

Table of Contents

Preface

It may take some time before young girls entering into womanhood understand who they are as women. After my husband graduated from seminary, he accepted a position as youth pastor at a church in downtown Los Angeles. One Sunday, an older woman introduced herself as I held our newborn son. She asked, "Do you play the piano." I said, "No, but my husband does." Then she asked, "Do you sing?" Again, I responded, "No, but my husband does." Then in a final effort to discover any gifts or talents, she asked, "Do you teach Bible studies?" Again, I repeated my answer, "No, but my husband does."

Although this woman tried to be friendly, I had the distinct impression that I was obviously not going to meet many people's expectations of a youth pastor's wife. On the outside, it appeared that I was neither trained nor talented. It would be several years before I discovered how God had gifted me and how He wanted me to minister. Today, I am no longer discouraged by this woman's questions and my apparent inadequacy. I am now confident in His calling upon my life and the gifts that He has bestowed upon me.

Many have been incorrectly taught regarding what the Bible teaches about the essence and ministry of women. This motivated me to go to seminary and study the Scriptures for myself in order to learn how to answer questions about women biblically.

I was frequently able to travel with my husband to teach overseas. We began ministering behind the Iron Curtain in 1984. I found that everywhere we traveled, women were eager to gather for Bible studies to learn the Word of God. Often, it was the first Bible study they had ever attended that was taught by a woman.

I also began to co-host my husband's live call-in radio program, "Questions and Answers," which focused on questions about the Bible. On the program, issues about the role of women have been a frequent topic over the years. Women often comment that they enjoy hearing a woman's viewpoint on these topics. It is my prayer that this book will not only answer questions women are asking but will turn them to the Lord and to the Word of God.

Introduction

Gullible? Naïve? Easily deceived? Is that what a woman is like? Culture and tradition impact society's beliefs about women. A woman's characteristics, roles, and even her gender are frequently debated. Bible passages on womanhood are often either ignored or interpreted differently by different people. A woman's role in the church and home continues to be one of the most disputed topics today.

Women are looking for a purpose in life. They want to be valued. But they are bombarded by the many voices that seem to pressure and influence them from every segment of society. Articles and books written about women's issues have often raised even more questions. A heated debate can almost always be expected when the subject of the equality of men and women is addressed. This reflects the growing development of seemingly endless views about women. Even the definition of a woman is sometimes questioned.

Since the Word of God endures forever (Matt. 24:35), tradition and popular views about women should be evaluated from the Scriptures. A careful study of the biblical passages relating to the role of women must be the foundation of the view of women.

One purpose of this book is to biblically address the commonly held false views about women. The Scriptures reveal that women are not weak or easily deceived. Eve's reputation has suffered. Her false portrayal continues to diminish a woman's significance.

God fashioned Eve, made her beautiful, and gave her a wonderful husband. But for her, all that wasn't enough. She wanted more. She wanted the one thing God said she couldn't have. So, she took the forbidden fruit and then gave some to Adam. Sometimes we don't realize the impact that we have on others. Eve not only influenced Adam, but her decision also affected the role of women today. So how do we discover our biblical role as we consider Eve's deception and sin? Well, unlike Eve, we better not listen to those around us instead of listening to God's Word. But it's amazing how many ways we allow others to define who we are.

Television and the Internet seem to have a tremendous impact on our beliefs. Wikipedia and Google answer our questions. Blogs and forums provide the setting for us to debate our opinions. Facebook, Instagram, TikTok, and X (Twitter) influence our social life.

Our culture impacts who we are as women. Some question Eve's humanity. Her role as helper continues to be demeaned. Her deception often erroneously defines her as one who is easily deceived. Her flawed character results in a distorted image of women.

As we walk through our own Garden of Eden, how can we understand who we are as women? Are we fully human? Are we equal to men? What is our role? What's a woman to do? Understanding our essence as designed by God is fundamental. It is the starting point in determining our personhood and our role as women. Knowing who we are must precede our search for what we should do. But where do we begin? A plethora of books, articles, and blogs have been written about women's issues, attempting to resolve the problems of women in today's world. But many have merely raised more questions.

There seems to be no clear-cut definition today of a woman's significance and role in society. For some, a successful career is their goal. Some prefer not to marry. Some are single mothers. Others may choose not to have children. Some may want to become transgender. They are bombarded by the many voices that seem to pressure and influence them in every segment of society.

What are the criteria for making wise choices? Since Eve's desire to make her own decisions in the Garden of Eden, women have been struggling for their independence and equality. This endeavor has often been met with resistance or the suppression of women. In the first century, Jewish historian Flavius Josephus claimed that the Scripture said, "A woman is inferior to her husband in all things."[1] Roman consul Marcus Porcius Cato (234-139 BC) argued against repealing laws that limited women's use of expensive goods, crying in response to their uprising, "as soon as they begin to be your equals, they will have become your superiors."[2]

Noting that women have been considered both physically and intellectually inferior historically, Columbia Encyclopedia explains, "Both law and theology had ordered their subjection. Women could not possess property in their own names, engage in business, or control the disposal of their children or even of their own persons."[3] But it would be several centuries before feminism as a movement would begin. Arising from eighteenth century humanism and the Industrial Revolution, feminism is defined as a "movement for the political, social, and educational equality of women with men."[4] In order to justify an opinion, it is easy to find someone who agrees with that viewpoint. But instead of debating the issues, we must be like the Bereans. These Jews in the synagogue of Berea held the Scriptures in such high regard that they even sought to verify the teachings of the Apostle Paul as he spoke in their synagogue. Luke praises the Bereans in Acts 17:11,

Now these were more noble-minded than those in Thessalonica, for they received the word with great eagerness, examining the Scriptures daily to see whether these things were so.

What wonderful models for women today! The Word of God is the only source of accuracy. His Word is truth. Every opinion and interpretation must be verified by Scripture or else rejected. Scripture must be used to define Scripture. A vague passage should be interpreted by evaluating clear teaching in other parts of the Bible.

Differing methods of interpreting Scripture have a decisive impact on one's understanding of the biblical role of women. Some hold to a broad, generalized interpretation of passages regarding the role of women, resulting in an overly strict, legalistic application. For example, some teach that 1 Timothy 2:11 prohibits women from leadership roles in the church, even over women and children. Others hold that the silence of women in the church (1 Cor. 14:34) is absolute, concluding that women should not even express their opinions in church meetings.

On the other end of the spectrum, women are ordained as pastors and elders. For some, gender is not an issue in church leadership. The publishing of egalitarian or gender-neutral Bibles reveals an inclination of some toward gender equality.

Answers to questions about the role of women must be expounded from the Scriptures, rather than being derived from tradition or society. One day as I was teaching a course on the biblical role of women in a Bible college, one of my students mentioned that her father, who was a pastor, had changed his opinion over several decades regarding the ministry of women in the church. She stated that he used to be extremely strict regarding the role of women in his church, but now his view had become much more liberal. What made him change? The same thing that formed his opinion originally—culture. His beliefs merely mirrored the views of society.

This book is not intended to be a rebuttal of the views of Christian egalitarians or legalistic complementarians. It is a biblical theology of the role of women. It begins with the role of Eve at creation and after the fall, then addresses the function of women in the Old Testament and at the time of Christ. The New Testament verses on the role of women in the church and home are then examined. A study of these passages will help bring understanding to the biblical role of women today. Headship and submission will be discussed, as well as the meaning of *weaker vessel.*

A biblical theology of the role of women as it is developed historically must begin with the careful application of the rules of biblical hermeneutics.[5] Unless the Word of God is believed to be the sole authority in the formulation of a doctrine on the role of women, both tradition and a postmodern society will continue to dictate attitudes and beliefs about women. As we will see, the creation of Eve as depicted in Genesis 1 and 2 is the background sketch from which the biblical portrait of a woman should be painted.

The early chapters of Genesis describe God's distinctive creation of Eve. Yet they also record her subsequent failure to fulfill His original plan. These chapters are foundational to women's issues today because they address such subjects as Eve being created in the image of God, male and female role distinctions, and the effects of the fall. A New Testament study of the role of women reveals references to Eve in 1 Corinthians 11:8-9. And 1 Timothy 2:13 challenges us to examine the creation and fall passages in the Book of Genesis.

Without an accurate understanding of Eve's humanity and role, New Testament passages relating to the character and responsibility of women can easily be misinterpreted or applied incorrectly. Eve is our prototype. Understanding her creation, her fall, and the consequences of her fall are critical. The Bible's definition of a woman empowers women today to live godly lives and fulfill their God-given purpose.

1

Uniquely Fashioned

In the book of Genesis, God begins to weave the tapestry of a woman. The design is intricate. The workmanship is exquisite. Eve is uniquely fashioned as a woman, distinct from her husband, Adam.

The Genesis record begins with the creation of the heavens and the earth. It must have been incredible to observe. It was a time when *the morning stars sang together and all the sons of God shouted for joy* (Job 38:7). Following the formation of the heavens and the earth, the Scriptures document the creation of the fish of the sea, the birds of the sky, and the animals of the earth. Then unexpectedly, the wording changes from *Let there be* to *Let us make* in Genesis 1:26-27 when God announces His final, highest creative act—making man in His own image. Then God said:

Let Us make man in Our image, according to Our likeness; and let them rule over the fish of the sea and over the birds of the sky and over the cattle and over all the earth, and over every creeping thing that creeps on the earth (Gen. 1:26).

It is apparent that the word *man* in Genesis 1:26 and 27 is a generic term for mankind because of the use of the word *them* in both verses. This is also substantiated using the Hebrew word *adam*, meaning, "a class of being created by God without regard to sex, with a focus as a class of creature, distinct from animals, plants, or even spiritual beings."[6]

The fulfillment of God's plan is realized in the next verse with the creation of Adam and Eve in the image of God. They were identical in essence, yet distinct physically. *God created man in His own image, in the image of God, He created him; male and female He created them* (Gen. 1:27). The image of God is not a physical likeness since God is spirit (John 4:24). Rather, the image of God consists of that which distinguishes man from the lower creation and enables man to have fellowship with God. It includes spirituality (immortality), personality (mind, volition, emotion, and self-consciousness), and initially being free of sin (Gen. 2:7, 15-25; Jam. 3:9).

Boa summarizes the distinctive creation of Adam and Eve as being "created primarily and ultimately for relationship with God."[7] None of the animals was created in God's image. This was a privilege reserved for Adam and Eve, making them unique—a higher and distinctive creation. They alone had the ability to have fellowship with Almighty God. We are so preoccupied with living that sometimes we forget the reason we were created. Fellowship with God should be our greatest priority. But is it first on our to-do list? Do we reflect on the ultimate purpose of the image of God in us?

Stitzinger summarizes the concept of the image of God:

> The image has to do with the ontological or spiritual qualities, namely, the communicable attributes that man and woman reflect from God. This is best understood as a moral, not a physical, likeness. The image of God is usually understood to include the will or freedom of choice, self-consciousness, self-transcendence, self-determination, rationality, moral discernment for good and evil, righteousness, holiness, and worship. Basically, it is that which makes men "persons."[8]

The words *image* and *likeness* in Genesis 1:26 are synonymous Hebrew parallelism rather than referring to two aspects of God's nature. The second adds emphasis to the first. Some have attempted to explain the terms theologically, stating that image denotes man's essence, which is unchangeable, and likeness refers to the changing part of man, which may be lost. But this is disproved by the interchangeable use of the words in Genesis 5:1 and 9:6. A distinction between these two terms must be rejected both exegetically and theologically.[9]

The male and female were a higher creation than the animals. But they were not a product of either atheistic or theistic evolution. They were created by a deliberate and willful act of God Himself. "The root *bārā* has the basic meaning 'to create.' It differs from *yāṣar* 'to fashion' in that the latter primarily emphasizes the shaping of an object while *bārā* emphasizes the initiation of the object."[10] "The word is used in the Qal [verb form] only of God's activity and is thus a purely theological term."[11] Creation was the sole handiwork of God Himself.

The theory of evolution is also contrary to the nature of God. It demeans His character. His justice demands retribution for sin in the form of death. If death already occurred prior to the sin of Adam and Eve, it would not be a penalty. It would simply be a natural occurrence. The practice of using nature or science to interpret the Word of God diminishes both the inspiration and the authority of Scripture.

Adam and Eve were each created in the image and likeness of God (Gen. 1:26). They were equal in essence, each possessing the capability for communion with God. There was no distinction between them in terms of their essential beings. Both were created in God's image, fully human.[12] Both were blessed by God (Gen. 1:28).

Although Adam and Eve were equal in personhood, they were unique in masculinity and femininity. The reference to male and female in Genesis 1:27 does not mean that each person has both male and female qualities. Nor can it be interpreted to imply that God is both male and female as some feminists assume. It simply means that when God created mankind, he made one man and one woman.

Together they were to rule over the earth and all its creatures. Sailhamer comments on what appear to be commands in the English translation of this verse,

> "The imperatives 'Be fruitful,' 'increase,' and 'fill' are not to be understood as commands in this verse since the introductory statement identifies them as a 'blessing.' The comparative, along with the jussive, is the common mood of the blessing (cf. Gen 27:19)." This dual responsibility reveals their superiority over the rest of creation.[13] But, as we will see, it does not prohibit any distinctiveness in their roles.

> *God blessed them; and God said to them, "Be fruitful and multiply, and fill the earth, and subdue it; and rule over the fish of the sea and over the birds of the sky and over every living thing that moves on the earth"* (Gen. 1:28).

Chapter two of Genesis describes in detail the general creation account of the previous chapter. This is not a second creation or a contradictory version, as some claim, but rather a more detailed description of the creation of

Adam and Eve. One cannot embrace the first account while rejecting the second. There were not two Adams and two Eves. There is no biblical evidence of any human being prior to the creation of Adam and Eve. Nor are there conflicting statements regarding the roles of Adam and Eve. Chapter one is merely an overview of creation; chapter two provides the details.

Genesis 2:7 states, *And the Lord God formed man of the dust of the ground, and breathed into his nostrils the breath of life; and man became a living soul.* This refutes the theory of the evolution of man. Although Adam was created from dust—worthless—he was given great value by God, created in His image and given life by His breath. With the breath of God, the clay became alive.

Adam was valued not by that of which he was made, but because of Who made him and what he became—a living soul. When the Scriptures in Genesis 1 speak of Adam and Eve being created in the image of God, the word *El* (a common name for God) is used to emphasize deity and power. But *El* is used in the plural, *Elohim*, likely referring to the Trinity.

In Genesis 2, when the Lord God is described as personally creating Adam and Eve, Jehovah is used emphasizing their relationship with God (Exo. 3:15). *Jehovah*, a name unique to the nation Israel,[14] appears eleven times in Genesis 2, emphasizing the fact that the Creator of the universe is the One who not only created Adam and Eve, but also had a relationship with them. This gives us the first glimpse in Scripture of a personal God, the One who cares for us.

In His infinite wisdom, God designed a plan for Adam and Eve that was unique to each of them. Although they were equal in their essence and in their relationship with God, Adam was designated as the head of the relationship. A denial of the headship of Adam prior to the fall is a result of an inadequate study of the first two chapters of Genesis.

Scriptural evidence of the headship of Adam, as ordained by God prior to the fall, is important considering the Christian feminists' teaching that male and female equality was lost at the fall and restored at the cross. This view teaches that the headship of man was a curse that resulted from sin, and therefore does not exist today either in the church or in the home.[15]

The authority and headship of man was designed by God before the sin of Eve and Adam. Man and woman were created equal in essence. Both were blessed by God. But their roles were distinct from the time of their creation.

Following the creation of the man, the Lord God places Adam in the "garden of Eden to cultivate it and keep it" (Gen. 2:15). In Genesis 2:16-17, God commands Adam not to eat from the tree of knowledge of good and evil,

The Lord God commanded the man, saying, "From any tree of the garden you may eat freely; but from the tree of the knowledge of good and evil you shall

not eat, for in the day that you eat from it you will surely die"

The authority of Adam is evident as God, prior to the creation of Eve, commands Adam not to eat of "the tree of the knowledge of good and evil." God tells Adam that the consequence of disobeying His command is death. As evidence of his higher creation, man was held morally accountable to God; the animals were not.[16] The actual translation of *you will surely die* is literally "dying, thou shalt die."[17] The likely theological meaning of this phrase is that they would die spiritually immediately (because of the sin of disobedience) and they would also die physically later. Spiritual death, "separation from God," would be immediate; physical death, or "cessation of life," would follow.[18] Both are the consequence of sin. Witmer explains, "God's penalty for sin was both spiritual and physical death (cf. Rom. 6:23; 7:13), and Adam and Eve…experienced both."[19]

Immediately after giving Adam the command not to eat of the tree of the knowledge of good and evil, God said, *It is not good for the man to be alone; I will make him a helper suitable for him* (Gen. 2:18).

God brought the animals to Adam for him to name them, but among the animals there was not a suitable helper for him. Perhaps the naming of the creatures revealed "his loneliness."[20] Following the failure to find a helpmate for Adam among the animals, Eve was created to fill a void in Adam's life.

At the end of each day of creation, God declared it to be good (Gen. 1:4, 10, 12, 18, 21, 25), but at the end of the sixth day of creation, with the creation of Adam and Eve, *God saw all that He had made, and behold, it was very good* (Gen. 1:31). Although Eve was created as a complement for Adam (Gen. 2:18-25), she was in no way inferior to him. God could have created both Adam and Eve out of the dust to designate their equality. But Eve was God's special gift to Adam. Her role as helper, *ezer,* rather than being demeaning, was positive and active. In John 14:16, 26, Jesus Christ predicts the coming of Holy Spirit and refers to Him as another comforter (Jesus being the other). The Greek word, *parakletos,* translated comforter, means "one called alongside to help."

Boa comments on Eve's role,

> "The emphasis here is on the woman's essential equality and compatibility with the man — her being 'fit' for him (vv. 18, 20)."[21] The use of the term helper in describing Eve, therefore, does not signify inferiority, weakness, or inadequacy. Women are created by God with great value. Their role as helper is given special significance by God's taking on the role of helper to the nation Israel, "Behold, God is my helper; The Lord is the sustainer of my soul'" (Psalm 54:4).

While basing Eve's role as helper on God functioning in a similar capacity, one cannot speculate that women are therefore superior to men. Helper is a role, not a divine attribute. God assumes many roles in Scripture. Agreeing that the role of helper in Genesis 2:18 cannot imply either inferiority or superiority, egalitarians erroneously conclude that men and women have a partnership characterized by equality in their roles.

Grounding her more restrictive definition of *ezer* on military language in the Old Testament rather than on the context of Genesis 2, James comments, "*Ezer* represents the strength and valor of a warrior. God created women to be warriors."[22] She concludes that she agrees with the woman who "didn't quite fit the 'helpmeet' mold," but preferred to be defined as a warrior.[23] The implication is that women can choose whichever meaning of *ezer* fits their personality.

After declaring Adam's need for a helpmeet, *The Lord God fashioned a rib, which He had taken from the man, into a woman and brought her to the man* (Gen. 2:22). The Hebrew word *banah* means "to build" and is contrasted with the forming or shaping of Adam out of the clay.[24] Adam's delight was apparent in verse 23 when he said, *This is now bone of my bones, And flesh of my flesh; She shall be called Woman, Because she was taken out of Man.*

The similarities and distinctions of Adam and Eve are apparent in the parallelism in this poetry. They are of the same flesh and the same bones, yet male and female. They are perfect complements.[25] Eve was not formed from the dirt like Adam; she was literally part of him. The English translation does not reveal the meaning and closeness of the Hebrew words: *Ish* for man and *Ishshah* (the feminine version of *Ish*) for woman. McComiskey explains,

> She is depicted as the physical counterpart of man, deserving of his unswerving loyalty. It is in this context (vv. 24–25) that the word is first used in the sense of 'mate' or 'wife.'[26]

The distinction in roles between Adam and Eve is further emphasized when the instructions for marriage specify that man is to be the initiator. *For this reason a man shall leave his father and his mother, and be joined to his wife; and they shall become one flesh* (Gen. 2:24). Even today, the man is usually the one who proposes.

It is the man that leaves his father and mother and clings to his wife. The result is that the two become one flesh. This verse also looks to the future where the relationship of a husband and wife would supersede and replace the parent-child bond. The highest priority would now be the relationship between the husband and wife. There needs to be a forsaking of dependence on parents. A new union has begun.

This introduces God's design for marriage—one man and one woman. Yet God's perfect plan was disrupted when sin entered the world.

The Choice To Sin

The third chapter of Genesis opens with a description of a snake or dragon, which is called a *serpent*. The Hebrew prime root *naw-khawsh´* means to hiss.[27] In Revelation 20:2, this crafty, unscrupulous serpent is referred to as *the dragon, the serpent of old, who is the devil and Satan.* It is not a coincidence that pagan religions, including the Canaanites, used a snake in their worship of Baal.[28]

Genesis 3:1 records the serpent's choice to tempt Eve rather than Adam. Understanding the reason for Satan deciding to tempt Eve is of vast importance. Was Eve easier to deceive, as many assume? Was she created with vulnerability in her nature?

The interpretation of this passage has implications for women today. If women are more easily deceived than men due to a weakness in their character, then the interpretation of all passages about women throughout the Bible will be affected. One's understanding of the biblical role of women will be tainted by the view that a vulnerability to deception is the chief underlying influence on a woman's behavior. If Genesis 3 isn't interpreted correctly, we won't interpret other passages about women correctly. The aroma of Eve's deception would permeate through the ages.

Strauch, in his otherwise excellent book, Equal Yet Different, believes that Satan approached Eve because she was "the more susceptible of the two to his subtle deceptions."[29]

Jamieson argues that her temptation was because "the subtle serpent knew that she was 'the weaker vessel.'"[30] Boa disagrees, stating,

> Eve was deceived, not because she was a woman and therefore more gullible, less intelligent, or less spiritually discerning, but because she chose to make such a radical decision without bringing the matter to her husband.[31]

Were these the reasons that the serpent spoke to Eve rather than to Adam? Did Satan assume that Eve would not consult either her husband or God? Was that his strategy? On the other hand, Satan's rationale was probably that Adam could not have been deceived because God spoke directly to him prior to Eve's creation. Adam knew what God said. But Eve had secondhand information. This fact, not a flaw in her character or womanhood, is what made her more vulnerable. Her deception is due to the situation and circumstances of her temptation, not a weakness in her being, as many assume.

The conversation between the serpent and Eve is based on hearsay, which is defined by the Federal Rules of Evidence as: "a statement, other than one made by the declarant while testifying at the trial or hearing, offered in evidence to prove the truth of the matter asserted."[32] The two witnesses are silent; neither God nor Adam speak. Since the Lord is the topic of the conversation, why does Eve not ask God directly what He had said? Especially when the serpent accuses God of lying (Gen. 3:4). Or why does she not ask her husband, who appears to be in proximity (v. 6)? Instead, Eve yields to the serpent's temptation to act independently of both God and her husband, Adam. Satan entices her into rejecting the role that God had designed for her. Her lack of firsthand knowledge made her vulnerable.

The erroneous view that women are more easily deceived continues today as seen in the following examples. In his commentary on 1 Timothy, Litfin agrees, stating, "Some chauvinists see Paul arguing here that women, as represented in their archetype Eve, are more gullible and thus more susceptible to error, than men."[33] It is not difficult to find a variety of flawed conclusions and applications regarding Eve's deception:

> Geneva Study Bible: "Adam was deceived, but through his wife's means, and therefore she is

worthily for this reason subject to her husband, and ought to be."[34]

Wesley's Notes: "She is more easily deceived, and more easily deceives."[35]

Commentary Critical and Explanatory on the Whole Bible: "The subtle serpent knew that she was "the weaker vessel" (1Pe 3:7). He therefore tempted her, not Adam.[36]

Harpers Bible Commentary: "Women are cautioned not to aspire to be teachers because, first, they are open to being led astray, as Eve was"[37]

The New Bible Commentary: Paul "sees some significance in the part Eve played in the fall and implies that all women have somehow inherited this disadvantage."[38]

The Commentary, Critical and Explanatory, on the Old and New Testaments: "Being more easily deceived, she more easily deceives [Bengel], (2Co 11:3)."[39]

Bible Readers Companion: "Paul then goes on to make the point that in the Fall Eve was deceived and seems to draw the conclusion that thus an authoritative teaching role is inappropriate."[40]

In Genesis 3:1, Satan shrewdly approaches Eve with a statement that implies God is unfair by restricting them from eating from every tree of the garden, *Indeed, has God said, "You shall not eat from any tree of the garden"*? Eve's response is accurate—almost. She explains that they can eat the fruit from all the trees of the garden except from "the fruit of the tree which is in the middle of the garden." She clearly understood that the penalty for eating of the tree of knowledge of good and evil would be death. However, perhaps to be certain to obey God's commandment, she adds the words *or touch it (Gen. 3:3)*.

While Satan questions God's word, Eve adds to it. Neither one is correct. God's Word is with exact quotes from Scripture (Matt. 4:4, 7, 10). The Bible contains warnings not to add to or take away from the Word of God (Deut. 4:2; Prov. 30:6; Rev. 22:18, 19). Walvoord states that "rejecting the Word of God is rejecting God Himself."[41]

Satan then contradicts God's pronouncement of impending death because of disobedience. God said, *You will surely die* (Gen. 2:27)," but the serpent told Eve, *You surely will not die!* (Gen. 3:4). That is the exact opposite of what God said. Satan apparently convinced Eve that God had deceived, misled, or even lied to Adam. Satan has been a liar from the beginning (John 8:44), and he cleverly deceives Eve into abandoning her role as helper, failing to trust either God or Adam. She clearly is acting on her own.

Just as Satan sinned by wanting to be like God (Isa. 14:14), so he tempts Eve in the same manner. He implies that God doesn't want them to eat from the tree of knowledge of good and evil because He knows that *in the day you eat from it your eyes will be opened, and you will be like God, knowing good and evil.* (Gen. 3:5). Apparently, Eve is convinced.

> *When the woman saw that the tree was good for food [lust of the flesh], and that it was a delight to the eyes [lust of the eyes], and that the tree was desirable to make one wise [pride of life], she took from its fruit and ate…* (Gen. 3:6).

Eve took the fruit of the tree and ate, but what about Adam? He was right there with Eve when Satan was talking to her (Gen. 3:6). Why didn't he speak up? Why didn't he protect her? He should have told her that God said not to eat of the fruit of the tree of the knowledge of good and evil. Why didn't Adam defend God when Satan accused Him of lying? God had given him the command before Eve was created, but the serpent persuaded Eve as Adam silently stood by. Then, without hesitation, Adam ate also. He yielded to temptation as well. He chose Eve over God.

This is interesting considering Genesis 1:28, which states that they were to rule over *every living thing that moves on the earth*. Rather than ruling, Adam and Eve both submitted to the serpent. As a result, sin entered the world—and death. Neil Armstrong's famous words when he first set foot on the moon on July 21, 1969, could certainly negatively be said of

Adam – "One small step for man, one giant leap for mankind." Adam's sin was an act with lasting consequences for all of God's creation. Paul recounts this event in Romans 5:12, *Therefore, just as through one man sin entered into the world, and death through sin, and so death spread to all men, because all sinned.*

The Greek *anthropos*, translated as *man* in Romans 5:12, could refer to mankind or humanity, [42] similar to the Hebrew *adam*, which can mean "man, mankind, Adam."[43] But Boa states that in this verse the word *anthropos* refers only to Adam. He continues,

> This is absolutely clear, since Paul goes on to identify the one man who sinned as "Adam" (v. 14) and to contrast his sin with the gift of righteousness which came by 'the one Man, Jesus Christ' (v. 15; cf. vv. 17-19). Paul draws the same contrast *between the man Adam and the man Jesus Christ in another epistle* (1 Cor. 15:21-22, 45).[44]

Greater culpability on Adam's behalf results from his greater responsibility. MacArthur explains the guilt of Adam: "Although he was not deceived by Satan, as was Eve, Adam still chose to disobey God. As the head of their relationship, he bore ultimate responsibility."[45]

This passage should challenge Christian women to stand firm in the Lord. Eve sinned first by listening to Satan and eating from the forbidden tree, and then by offering its fruit to Adam. The lesson for women today is that we must be alert to resist temptation to sin. We must also be careful of the ways in which we influence others. Are we a stimulus for good or for evil? Do we encourage others to walk with the Lord and obey Him? Or do we entice them to sin?

It is amazing to realize the influence we have on those whom God has put in our lives, especially those who are closest to us. We have a grave responsibility to be strong in the Lord personally and to become a catalyst for others to grow in Christ. This is an instance in Scripture where we can learn from a bad example. Instead of following in Eve's footsteps, we must resist temptation and seek God's will through the filling of the Holy Spirit. Only then will we glorify God and fulfill the plan He designed for us.

Adam bore the responsibility for sin for the entire human race, which indicates his headship of all mankind (Rom. 5:12; 1 Cor. 15:21-22). Yet Eve also bore responsibility for her sin (3:10, 16), and the serpent was cursed. As foretold in the commandment to Adam, there would be a penalty for sin—death. The implications of spiritual death would be seen immediately as Adam and Eve "hid themselves from the presence of the LORD God" (Gen. 3:8). When questioned by God about eating the forbidden fruit, Adam blames Eve; Eve blames the serpent. There was no confession or acknowledgement of sin. Aren't we guilty of the same thing today? It is tempting to blame someone else when we sin, rather than confess our sin to the Lord.

In Genesis 3:14-19, the consequences of sin are specified, first for the serpent, then for Eve, and finally for Adam. But amid a passage detailing the curse on the serpent is a prophecy of the hostility between Satan and the seed of the woman, *And I will put enmity between you and the woman, And between your seed and her seed; He shall bruise you on the head, And you shall bruise him on the heel* (Gen. 3:15).

This verse states that the hostility would be between Satan and the woman, and then between their offspring. But then the hostility is narrowed. The seed of the woman is defined in the masculine singular, *he,* whereas the seed of the serpent is replaced with *you.* The enmity becomes personal, not just between the seed of the woman, "the Promised One, the coming Messiah of Israel,"[46] and the serpent's seed, but the serpent himself.[47]

Keathley summarizes the significance of this passage to the virgin birth of Jesus,

> Though perhaps not understood then, we have in Genesis 3:15 the anticipation of the virgin birth. Satan's defeat and that of his seed (the unbelieving world) would come from the seed of the woman. It speaks of her seed, not his (the man's) nor theirs (the man and the woman). Deliverance would come from the woman without the aid of a man. The virgin birth of Jesus was vital since Romans 5:12 clarifies that the sin nature of humanity is passed through Adam. Therefore, just as through one man

sin entered into the world, and death through sin, and so death spread to all men, because all sinned—[48]

The virgin birth was prophesied by Isaiah: *Therefore the Lord Himself will give you a sign: Behold, the virgin shall conceive and bear a Son, and shall call His name Immanuel* (Isaiah 7:14).

The particulars of how the virgin birth would occur are found in Luke 2:35 as the angel Gabriel speaks to Mary while she is still a virgin: *The Holy Spirit will come upon you, and the power of the Most High will overshadow you; and for that reason the holy Child shall be called the Son of God.* Although Eve sinned, God would sovereignly choose a woman to bear the Son of God--evidence of His grace and a blessing for all the nations.

The consequences of the fall for Eve, stated in Genesis 3:16, differed from those which Adam was to experience. The Lord God spoke specifically to the woman, saying, *"I will greatly multiply your pain in childbirth, in pain you will bring forth children."*

It was predicted that the woman's pain in childbirth and bringing forth children, likely the "entire process of childbirth and child rearing,"[49] would bring hardship and distress.[50]

Verse 16 continues, *Yet your desire will be for your husband, And he will rule over you. Desire* is sometimes interpreted as a woman's intense love for her husband. Why did Eve not have this desire for Adam when she was first created? Why would God give a good consequence for an evil act? It is vital to understand that the context of this passage is the penalty for sin. This is the punishment phase of the trial. This same Hebrew word *desire* in Genesis 4:7 denotes an "attempt to usurp or control."[51] We get an idea of the impending battle for control between Adam and Eve as we read of the struggle between Cain and sin.

Keil and Delitsch explain the meaning of the Hebrew word for desire,

> [Eve] was punished with a desire bordering upon disease (תְּשׁוּקָה from שׁוּק to run, to have a violent craving for a thing), and with subjection to the man. "And he shall rule over thee." Created for the man, the woman was made subordinate to him from the very first; but the supremacy of the man was not intended to become a despotic rule, crushing the woman into a slave…[52]

Commenting on Genesis 3:16, the Net Bible translator note states: "The Hebrew verb מָשַׁל (*mashal*) means 'to rule over,' but in a way that emphasizes powerful control, domination, or mastery. This also is part of the baser human nature." Then the translator adds, "the Lord simply announces the struggle without indicating who will emerge victorious."[53] In keeping with this interpretation, Net Bible translates Genesis 3:16b, "You will want to control your husband, but he will dominate you."[54]

The context of the passage is the curse of the serpent and the punishment of Adam and Eve. The honeymoon is over. Sin has consequences. None of them is good. The definition of desire as a wife's love for her husband can in no way be construed as punishment. As a penalty for sin against God, would Adam now be rewarded with a loving and adoring wife? The context is what ultimately determines the meaning of a word. This is not a passage on the loving relationship of Adam and Eve. This is after the Fall. This is the punishment for their sin, not a blessing for good behavior. The battle has begun.

The husband's tendency to dominate his wife is part of the judgment of God. It is not the initiation of the headship of man. Nor is it the prolonging of the roles assumed in the fall—Eve as dominant and Adam as passive. Rather it is a distortion of the roles because of their sin, which results in a power struggle.

Kassian concludes,

> The best interpretation of the desire-rule clause is that after the Fall, women would rebel against their designated role and that men would abuse their role of leadership, thus creating tension in the male-female relationship.[55]

The Christians for Biblical Equality reject the headship and authority of Adam prior to the fall. Without any scriptural documentation, their Statement on Men, and Women, and Biblical Equality states,

> The Bible teaches that the rulership of Adam over Eve resulted from the Fall and was therefore not a part of the original created order. Genesis 3:16 is a prediction of the effects of the Fall rather than a prescription of God's ideal order.[56]

Genesis 3:16 does not redefine the marriage roles because of the fall. Boa explains that it is "not a *prescription* for marriage, but a description of one of the unfortunate effects of the Fall."[57] The headship of Adam was not instigated as part of the curse of sin. Genesis records the authority God gave Adam, beginning at creation and continuing after the fall.

Genesis 1 and 2 document the authority and leadership of Adam as designed by God prior to the fall. The Apostle Paul notes that "man was not created for the woman's sake, but woman for the man's sake (1 Cor. 11:9) and that "it was Adam who was first created, and then Eve" (1 Tim. 2:13). Although he mentions that Eve was deceived (1 Tim. 2:14), he doesn't talk of a change in roles. Man and woman were created equal in essence. Both were blessed by God. But their roles were distinct from the time of their creation.

The result of sin is a corruption of Adam and Eve's God-given roles. Headship did not begin after the fall. It is not a curse. Nor was Eve's subjection "the consequence of her being deceived," as Jamieson holds.[58] In essence, their roles are the same after the fall, but their now sinful natures would be tempted to distort their roles.

Satan and the ground are cursed; Adam and Eve are not personally cursed. In Deuteronomy 28, blessings that will come because of obedience are contrasted with the curses that will come upon disobedient Israel. Deuteronomy 28:45 warns:

So all these curses shall come on you and pursue you and overtake you until you are destroyed, because you would not obey the Lord your God by keeping His commandments and His statutes which He commanded you.

The issue is obedience to the Lord. There are always consequences for sin. The consequences for Adam and Eve are stated in Genesis 3:17 and 18. Likewise, there are always blessings for those who obey God.

The result of God's judgment for sin is that there is now conflict where there was harmony; competition where there was unity. The now corrupt natures of Adam and Eve, acquired as a result of their sin, will seek to dictate their lives as Satan continues to influence God's creation. Yet throughout the Bible, there are accounts of women who were greatly used by God in spite of the curse. We have this same choice today. Are we going to let our lives be controlled by God so we honor Him, or will we yield to sin?

3

Women in Israel

The authority that was first given to Adam continued throughout the Old Testament as God consistently designated men to be the leaders in Israel. Although Moses exhibited great faith as God's servant in leading His people out of Egypt, the task of judging the people in the wilderness became a demanding responsibility. Following the godly advice of his father-in-law, Moses chose able men, not women, as heads and leaders of the people (Exo. 18:17-27). This allowed Moses to teach the Israelites the law and provide guidance for everyday life. The men selected by Moses judged the minor disputes, thereby lessening his burden of leadership.

In Exodus 28:41, the sons of Aaron were ordained and consecrated so they could serve the Lord as priests. Although the priesthood resided solely within the tribe of Levi by a perpetual statute, it was only the sons, not the daughters, who were chosen to minister to the Lord and intercede for the nation. Prior to the institution of the priesthood, it was the father, as the head of the family, who served as priest (Gen. 31:54; Job 1:5).

Miriam. Although men were designated by God as leaders of Israel in the Old Testament, many women were used by God and exhibited strong faith. Miriam, the sister of Moses, was a prophetess in Israel. When she was young, her mother entrusted her to watch her baby brother, Moses, when he was hidden from the Pharaoh in the reeds along the banks of the Nile (Exo. 2:1-8). When Pharoah's daughter discovered Moses, Miriam courageously offered to find a nurse for him so Pharaoh's daughter could later claim him as her son. This allowed Moses' mother to care for Moses as an infant and actually receive compensation as his nurse. Miriam later encouraged Israel to sing praises to the Lord (Exo. 15:20-21). But then she decided she wanted more. Numbers 12:1-20 records the rebellion of Miriam, the prophetess, and her brother Aaron, high priest of Israel.

The Lord rebuked Miriam and Aaron when they spoke against Moses and were jealous of God speaking through him. A case of sibling rivalry had developed. The Lord overheard their complaint. Suddenly the Lord ordered Moses, Aaron, and Miriam to go out to the tent of meeting. It was like being called to the principal's office. They knew they were in trouble.

Notice the order of names in Numbers 12:1. It was Miriam and Aaron who spoke against Moses, implying that she was the leader of this rebellion. However, when the Lord speaks to them, He puts them in order of His choosing: Moses (leader of Israel), Aaron (High Priest of Israel), and Miriam (prophetess) (v. 4). The Lord's words and actions in the next few verses bear out His sovereignly chosen chain-of-command in Israel.

The Lord appeared in a "pillar of cloud and stood at the doorway of the tent" (12:5). The Lord then called to Aaron and Miriam. When they approached the Lord, He said,

Hear now My words: If there is a prophet among you, I, the Lord, shall make Myself known to him in a vision. I shall speak with him in a dream. Not so, with My servant Moses, He is faithful in all My household; With him I speak mouth to mouth, Even openly, and not in dark sayings, And he beholds the form of the Lord. Why then were you not afraid to speak against My servant, against Moses? (Num. 12:6-8).

The Lord explained that his relationship with Moses was above that of a prophet, or a prophetess like Miriam. Notice that the Lord did not say, "If there is a woman among you." This was not an issue of gender, but rather leadership as appointed by God. Miriam and Aaron should have been afraid to speak against Moses, the chosen servant of Jehovah. God explained that He spoke directly to Moses, but to the prophets (a direct reference to Miriam) He used dreams, visions, and riddles. He then reproved them both for daring to speak against Moses.

This was a case of a prophetess and the high priest of Israel attempting to undermine the ministry of their younger brother, Moses, whom the Lord called "My servant" (v. 8). God Himself had chosen Moses as Israel's leader. Aaron was the high priest. Miriam was a prophetess. Yet Moses was selected by God as the leader of Israel, the one with whom He spoke face to face. But Miriam and Aaron were jealous of Moses, complaining that God could just as easily have spoken through them.

Then the anger of the Lord burned against Aaron and Miriam, making her leprous. The judgment was harsh. But was it fair? What about Aaron? The use of Miriam's name first in Numbers 12:1, as well as the Hebrew verb speak occurring in the feminine singular,[59] implies that Miriam was the instigator of this rebellion. It is apparent that she is the one who bore the punishment for their sin. It is also significant that if Aaron had been struck with leprosy, he could not have performed his duties as high priest of Israel (Lev. 22:2-3).

As a priest, Aaron would have been familiar with leprosy and realized the seriousness of the deformity and social isolation associated with this illness. Aaron then begged Moses not to hold them accountable for their sin. Aaron the high priest, the one chosen by God to intercede for the nation Israel and offer sacrifices for their sins, was not the one to pray for Miriam. It was Moses who prayed for her healing. God answered Moses' prayer and, following a week of isolation outside the camp, Miriam was healed. The entire nation Israel had to wait seven days until God was through punishing Miriam for her sin of attempting to usurp Moses' authority.

Satan wanted to be like God (Isa. 14:14). Miriam wanted to be like Moses. They were not content with their God-given roles. Although the account of Miriam's rebellion against Moses was not described as a gender issue, it is an example of a woman claiming equality with a male leader designated by God. It should serve as warning to women that they should not attempt to claim authority that has not been given to them by the Lord.

This incident seems to be an example of God confirming the leadership and authority that He had established in Israel through Moses. This was a warning to Israel not to question God's hierarchy of leadership in the nation. Whatever our reasoning, we are not to superimpose our desires upon God's sovereign plan. Women, as well as men, are responsible to follow God's design of leadership.

Deborah. In contrast to Miriam's self-willed rebellion and attempt to usurp authority, Deborah neither sought nor desired authority that was not given to her by God. She was one of those raised up by God to be a judge in Israel (cf. Jud. 2:16). Deborah, the wife of Lappidoth, was a prophetess who judged Israel (Jud. 4:4) during a time when "there was no king in Israel; everyone did what was right in his own eyes" (Jud. 21:25). This was a period of rebelliousness in Israel when unlikely leaders were used of God to judge the nation. Although the word *judge* can also be translated *govern* or *rule*, the depiction of Deborah sitting under a tree in the hill country of Ephraim, rather than in the city gate of Jerusalem, is a picture of counsel rather than national leadership. It appears that her judging was private, rather than public; local rather than national: *She used to sit under the palm tree of Deborah between Ramah and Bethel in the hill country of Ephraim; and the sons of Israel came up to her for judgment* (Jud. 4:5).

Deborah is said to have judged Israel for forty years. God raised her up as a judge in response to Israel crying out to the Lord following twenty years of severe oppression by Jabin, king of Canaan.

In her role as prophetess, Deborah sent for Barak and prophesied to him God's instructions in leading the army of Israel. Through Deborah, the Lord God of Israel commanded Barak to take ten thousand men to Mount Tabor to fight against Sisera, the commander of the army of Jabin, King of Canaan. Deborah prophesied the defeat of Sisera. However, Barak refused to follow God's orders unless Deborah accompanied him.

> *Then Barak said to her, "If you will go with me, then I will go; but if you will not go with me, I will not go." She said, "I will surely go with you; nevertheless, the*

honor shall not be yours on the journey that you are
about to take, for the Lord will sell Sisera into the
hands of a woman" (Judges 4:8, 9).

Because of Barak's refusal to assume this leadership role
without a woman going with him, God gave the honor of
the victory to a woman rather than to him (v. 15). Barak
then led the battle with ten thousand men against Sisera, the
commander of the Canaanite king, and his army. But Sisera
escaped and a woman named Jael killed him with a tent
peg (v. 21). It is likely that Deborah composed the song of
praise to the Lord, God of Israel, that was sung by Deborah
and Barak (Judges 5:7). Following the defeat of Sisera, the
land of Israel was *"undisturbed for forty years"* (Judges 5:31).

Deborah was a godly woman in a time of rebellion and
ungodliness. She is an example of faithfulness in fulfilling
the ministry that God designated for her. She was willing
to play a supportive role and did not attempt to take either
authority or honor for herself. When we fulfill the role God
intended for women, He will use us mightily as well.

Ruth. The faith of Ruth the Moabitess is contrasted to the
rebellion of Israel during the time of the Judges. The events
in the Book of Ruth provide a glimmer of hope during this
time when Israel was characterized by apostasy. In an era
of decadence and rebellion, the story of Ruth and Boaz
reveals the sovereign work of a faithful God to the believing

remnant in Israel. Boaz's role as kinsman-redeemer for Ruth is a type of the Lord Jesus Christ as our redeemer.

The Lord God of Israel used a gentile maiden from an idolatrous, pagan nation, who married a Hebrew, to be in the line of King David. The blessing of the Lord on this faithful line of Israel, through whom the Messiah would come, provides further condemnation on His rebellious people. God will always work through those who are faithful to Him. Boaz praises Ruth, saying, *May the Lord reward your work, and your wages be full from the Lord, the God of Israel, under whose wings you have come to seek refuge* (Ruth 2:12).

The Book of Ruth is a witness of God's sovereignty and providence, which are coupled with His lovingkindness as He brings both famine and food, as well as rest and blessing. Ruth's devotion to Naomi is an example of submission. Her faith is rewarded by an impartial God. The book reveals that the kingship of David is a fulfillment of the promise given to Judah.[60]

When the nation Israel rejected God's theocratic rule, the Lord chose a man to reign as king over them (Deut. 17:14-15; 1 Sam. 9:16-17; 15:1). Because of Saul's disobedience, God then selected David, commanding the prophet Samuel to anoint him as king (1 Sam. 16:12). Men, not women, were anointed by God to reign over Israel (Psa. 132:17; 1 Sam. 12:13; 15:1).

The Proverbs 31 woman. Wisdom is personified as a woman in Proverbs 1–9. In Proverbs 31, a woman is honored for her virtue. Her qualities come to light as the crowning touch of this book of wisdom. She is the counterpart to the mighty man of valor—warrior of Israel. As the courageous hero is indispensable to the nation Israel, so the virtuous woman is to the home. The king depended on the warrior; her husband trusted in her. He provided strength in war; she imparted strength of character. He was clothed in crimson; she was adorned in scarlet. He conquered a nation; she managed a household. He surveyed a battlefield; she selected a vineyard. He was honored by a nation; she was praised by her family. She was characterized by wisdom and managed her home well. The basis of her wisdom was her fear of the Lord. She was the Mary/Martha of the Old Testament. Her faith was combined with good deeds and her loving care of her family. She receives the praise of not only her family, but also the entire community.

In contrast to this woman, Athaliah is an example of a woman who rebelled against God's plan for Israel. The daughter of Jezebel and Ahab, she was the only ruling queen of Judah. She destroyed all the royal sons except Joash, who was hidden from her. She reigned over the land of Judah for six years until the high priest ordered that she be put to death (2 Kings 11:1-20).

Huldah. The account of Huldah, the prophetess, is recorded in 2 Kings 22:8–20. In the eighteenth year of Josiah's reign over Judah, a copy of the Book of the Law was discovered during the renovation of the temple in Jerusalem. The Law had been lost and neglected in Israel, and King Josiah tore his clothes in mourning when he realized how the people of Israel had neglected God's Word. Josiah commanded Hilkiah the high priest and four of his officers to inquire of the Lord concerning the Word of God. Huldah was personally selected by these men and was used of the Lord to foretell the impending disaster that would come upon Jerusalem and the disobedient people of Judah. Because of Josiah's tender heart and humility, Huldah prophesied that God would spare him from seeing the evil that He would bring on Jerusalem. When the lost book of the law was found, the prophetess Huldah was consulted rather than Jeremiah or Zephaniah, her contemporaries. Her word was accepted by all as divinely revealed (2 Kgs 22:14–20; 2 Chr 34:22–28) and led to a revival.[61]

It is interesting that when King Josiah said to inquire of the Lord, the High Priest went to a woman. Although she apparently was not a leader, she had a reputation in the city as one through whom God spoke. Josiah did not question her prophecy but responded by making a covenant to obey God. This was approximately five years after the beginning of Jeremiah's prophetic ministry.

Over time Israel was made more vulnerable because of the nation's rebelliousness and the failure of her prophets, priests, and kings to be faithful to the Lord. The nation went astray, practiced idolatry, and was conquered by foreign powers. God pronounces judgment on His people in Isaiah 3:12, stressing the lack of godly male leadership (cf.

Nahum 3:13), *O My people! Their oppressors are children, and women rule over them.* The reference to women may mean that wives were influencing their husbands who were rulers, or that the male leaders lacked vigor.[62]

Esther. The absence of the name of God in the Book of Esther has caused many to doubt God's hand upon its main characters, Esther and Mordecai for centuries. But the Book of Esther is like an unsigned painting, challenging us to search its pages to discover the existence of the One who remains elusive. By avoiding any reference to His being, God has succeeded in calling even greater attention to His work. Rather than being an oversight, the omission of His name is evidence of His providence. God chose to omit His name, knowing that He doesn't need credentials or valida-tion. *The heavens declare His righteousness* (Ps. 97:6) and His works among the children of men reveal His presence. His being is discreetly revealed through His faithfulness to Israel (Ps. 98:2,3).

Following the return of a remnant to Jerusalem and the rebuilding of the temple, Esther, a young Jewish orphan, became queen of the great Persian Empire (Est. 2:17). The obedience Esther learned as a child prepared her to be used by God to intercede for the Jews, saving the nation from a destruction that could have prevented the birth of the Messiah.[63] Her godly qualities of humility, wisdom, and faithfulness are clearly shown throughout the book that bears her name. She is an example of a woman who integrated submission and leadership under God's direction.

Mordecai recognizes the providence of God by suggesting that the deliverance of the Jews could very well be the reason why God elevated Esther to the position of queen.

> *For if you remain silent at this time, relief and deliverance will arise for the Jews from another place and you and your father's house will perish. And who knows whether you have not attained royalty for such a time as this?* (Est. 4:14).

Esther's bravery is evident as she risks her life to gain an audience with the king and plead with him for the nation Israel. Israel will be delivered. The only question is whether or not Esther will be the one who will be influential in its deliverance. God's plan will be accomplished. Obedience to God makes us available to be used by Him. If we refuse to obey Him, He will simply use someone else. But we will miss the blessing.

4

A New Era

The New Testament honors women in many significant ways. The incarnation of God's Son began in the womb of a woman (Gal. 4:4). During His ministry, Jesus often demonstrated His love and concern for women. Mary and Martha were among His closest friends (John 11:5). He revealed His Messiahship to a woman of Samaria (John 4:26). Jewish men were discouraged from talking with woman in public, even their own wives, yet Jesus often spoke publicly to women. Although Jewish women "were discouraged from studying the law, Jesus taught them alongside men (Mt. 14:21; 15:38; etc.)."[64] During His agony on the cross, He provided for the care of His mother by the Apostle John (John 19:26). After His resurrection, His first appearance was to a woman from whom He had exorcised seven demons (Mark 16:9). It was to this woman that Jesus entrusted the news of His resurrection, which she was to deliver to His disciples. Jesus' love and respect for women is evident. However, women were not among the twelve that Jesus chose as His disciples.

In Luke 10:32-38 when Mary was sitting at Jesus' feet to listening to his teaching, she was "assuming the role of a rabbinical student, a role reserved in Judaism exclusively for men."[65] Priscilla, who was part of a husband-wife team with Aquila, privately explained to Apollos "the way of God more accurately" (Acts 18:26). Lydia of Thyatira, the first recorded European believer, was a seller of purple in whose home Paul and Barnabas stayed (Acts 16:14–15); prominent women of Thessalonica and Berea were among the first believers in those cities (Acts 17:4, 12); and Euodia and Syntyche were women who Paul said, "shared in my struggle in the gospel" (Phil. 4:2–3). A prayer meeting was held in the home of Mary, the mother of John Mark (Acts 12:12). Churches met in the homes of Nymphas (Col. 4:15), Philemon's wife, Apphia (Phlm. 2), and Priscilla (1 Cor. 16:19).

Salvation through faith in Jesus Christ is available to all who believe (John 3:16). Men and women are individually responsible to believe in Christ for the forgiveness of sins. At the moment of salvation, every believer, male or female, is indwelt with the Holy Spirit and placed into the body of Christ (1 Cor. 12:13). A woman who has trusted in Christ for her salvation is totally and completely accepted by God. Galatians 3:28 teaches that women are equal with men in their position in Christ. The issue in this verse is theological, not experiential. The context of Galatians 3:28 is justification by faith. This passage teaches spiritual equality, which must be distinguished from role equality. The death and resurrection of Jesus Christ did not change or eliminate role distinctions that were initiated in the Garden of Eden prior to the fall.

Galatians 3:28 does not teach that all differences of nationality, status, and sex cease to exist at conversion. It is an error to say that "one in Christ" means that there are no distinctions within the body of Christ. Within the Church, the One Body of Christ, there are saved Jews and saved Gentiles. Salvation does not do away with one's nationality. Salvation also does not change one's work situation. Paul gave instructions to Christian slaves to obey their masters (cf. Eph.6:5-8). Paul told slaves to not be concerned about their status, but to pursue freedom if possible (1 Cor.7:21-23). Neither does salvation affect one's gender.

What Paul is saying in Galatians 3:28 is that there is an equal standing before God for three specific groups: Jewish Christians and Gentile Christians, Christians who are slaves and Christians who are free, and male Christians and female Christians (cf. 1 Cor. 12:13.) Oneness in Christ does not eliminate these distinctions. Neither did Adam and Eve being created in the image of God exclude their role designations.

It is the context of a passage, not culture or personal viewpoints, which ultimately determines the meaning of the text. Melick comments on the importance of correct contextual analysis in understanding Galatians 3:28.

> This is a soteriological statement: it speaks to the doctrine of salvation. The teaching is that all believers, without regard to social distinctions, have equal access to God through Christ, and, consequently, are to be unified in the Body of Christ.[66]

Those who fail to understand the theological meaning of equality in Christ in Galatians 3:28 often accuse the Apostle Paul of teaching conflicting views on women. Or they may question the inspiration of Scripture. This verse is probably one of the most frequently misinterpreted and misused verses in the Bible concerning the topic of male and female roles. Melick argues against a faulty application of Galatians 3:28, stating that it is a mishandling of the Scripture to define church leadership based on passages addressing salvation: "While Paul clearly affirms the equality of men and women in salvation, he equally and just as clearly affirms the priority of men in church leadership."[67]

This text does advocate male and female equivalence, documenting an equality of status in Christ. However, it does not endorse role equality in either the church or the home. To attempt to apply this passage to women's roles in the church or home takes the verse out of context and diminishes the argument for justification by faith alone.

In the body of Christ, there are no divisions or distinctions. God has no favorites, no preferences. All who come by faith are equally accepted. This is not a verse about relationships; it is a verse about a believer's acceptance by God and His unifying work within the body of Christ. We are all equally children of God through faith in Christ Jesus.

Christian feminists erroneously use Galatians 3:28 as the basis of their philosophy of functional equality in the home and in the church, but the theological concept of "in Christ" refers to equality within the spiritual body of Christ. The Body of Christ is a metaphor for the universal church (Eph. 1:22-23), of which Christ is the head (Eph. 5:23). Equality within this universal church refers to the equal status of all believers in their standing before God. Each and every believer is fully accepted by God at the point of salvation. Equality in Christ is all-inclusive—no believer is excluded. There is to be no discrimination in the Body of Christ regarding race, social status, or gender. Although all believers are equal positionally "in Christ," Scripture does not teach that all believers have the same functions within the local church.

The application of this verse is that contrary to social prejudice and discrimination, a Gentile woman slave is considered by God to be equal positionally in Christ to a Jewish male slave owner. This is borne out in the book of Philemon. The Apostle Paul writes this letter to a slave owner in the Colossian church after his runaway slave, Onesimus was led to Christ by Paul during his imprisonment in Rome (Philem. 10).

Although the Apostle considered Onesimus to be a brother in the Lord (v. 16), Paul sent him back to Philemon as a slave who was now a beloved brother to them both. Paul asked Philemon to accept Onesimus as he would the Apostle Paul, requesting that any debt owed by the slave be charged to the apostle. Acknowledging that although there is no distinction in Christ between slave and freeman (Col. 3:11), Paul instructed the believers who were slaves to obey their masters, *working heartily, as for the Lord rather than for men* (Col. 3:2).

There also is no distinction between men and women in the body of Christ. Women are among the saints who are to be equipped for *the work of service* and for *the building up of the Body of Christ* (Eph. 4:12). All of the commands to believers in the New Testament include women, who are an essential part of the Body of Christ. Women in the New Testament times were greatly involved in ministry.

The fact that God did not select women for leadership in either the nation Israel or the New Testament churches does not imply their inferiority. They are not valued less because of this distinction. God's plan for women has been uniquely designed and implemented, beginning with the creation of Eve. It encompasses every era and reveals God's loving purpose for women in each culture. This is evident as we look at Paul's instructions to Corinthian believers in the first century A.D.

The Issue of
Head Coverings

1 Corinthians 11:3-6

But I want you to know that Christ is the head of every man, and the man is the head of a woman, and God is the head of Christ. Every man who has something on his head while praying or prophesying disgraces his head. But every woman who has her head uncovered while praying or prophesying disgraces her head, for she is one and the same as the woman whose head is shaved. For if a woman does not cover her head, let her also have her hair cut off; but if it is disgraceful for a woman to have her hair cut off or be shaved, let her cover her head.

In 54-55 A.D., the Apostle Paul wrote an epistle to address questions raised by Corinthian believers. Paul challenges Christians in this problem-riddled first century church to abandon the divisions and immorality in their midst. His exhortations to unity and purity are grounded in positional sanctification—their standing in Jesus Christ because of their salvation. Lives of believers are to reflect their relationship with Jesus Christ. On two occasions, the Apostle addresses women's conduct in the Corinthian church. In chapter eleven, he confronts the issue of head coverings as a cultural symbol of submission. Although head coverings are not in use everywhere in the world today, the principles that Paul presents in this passage can be applied to all believers. In chapter fourteen, he tells women to keep silent in church.

Idolatry is condemned in chapter ten as Paul states that the goal in his life is to glorify God (1 Cor. 10:31). At the conclusion of chapter ten, Paul lists four specific factors for the Corinthian believers to consider in determining their behavior.

> *Whether, then, you eat or drink or whatever you do, do all to the glory of God. Give no offense either to Jews or to Greeks or to the church of God; just as I also please all men in all things, not seeking my own profit but the profit of many, so that they may be saved* (1 Cor. 10:31-33).

The most important aspect is that all be done to the glory of God. That is the first criterion in making a decision regarding any action. The Corinthian Christians were not to do something that would offend unbelievers (Jews or Greeks at that time) and therefore be a hindrance to the gospel. They were to take care not to offend or be a stumbling block to believers (the church of God) in such a way that would cause them to sin. Nothing was to be done out of selfishness or for personal profit, but rather their goal should be to win others to Christ.

These verses become the background for Paul's discussion on head coverings. In 1 Corinthians 11:2-16, Paul introduces the subject of headship, which is a very important issue today in debates on the role of women.

In verse 3, Paul states that *Christ is the head of every man, and the man is the head of a woman.*[68] But it does not say man is the head of every woman. Nor does it say that man is the head of women. It uses the singular, *a woman*, meaning a wife, not women in general.

In the discussion of the roles of headship, Cottrell notes the correlation between types of headship:

In the first relationship, Christ is the model for man's role as the head of the woman; in the second relationship, Christ is also the model for the woman's role as subordinate to the man. Thus Christ, in his incarnate state and in his role as Redeemer, becomes the model for both men and women, since he is the head of every man and at the same time subordinate to God the Father.[69]

Paul's example of God as the head of Christ is a proto-type of the Trinity possessing a hierarchy among equals. The Trinity provides the model of headship in this passage. God the Father and God the Son are equal in deity, yet they are distinct in respect to authority and role. Authority is given to the Son by the Father (Psa. 8:6; Mat. 28:18; 1 Cor. 15:27; Eph. 1:22; Heb. 2:6-8). Yet the Son willingly submits to the Father (Luke 22:42). Knight comments, "The headship of God in relation to the incarnate Christ in no way detracts from or is detrimental to His person as incarnate deity."[70]

Headship does not imply superiority, nor does sub-mission denote inferiority. Jesus Christ, who is deity, ful-filled both roles. Headship, therefore, does not need to be denounced or explained away to elevate women or prove their equality. Headship indicates the role of the husband, not his superiority as a person.

Although the context of this passage, as well as New Testament usage, argues for κεφαλή (*kephale*, head) meaning authority, some contend that it means source or origin, rejecting any notion of male authority in either the home or the church. Regarding the meaning of κεφαλή as source or origin, there is "no clear example in the time of the New Testament, even though feminists have gone to great pains to seek to find such usage."[71]

According to Grudem, his survey of 2,336 instances of *head* being interpreted as authority is:

> Probably sufficient to demonstrate that 'source, origin' is nowhere clearly attested as a legitimate meaning for κεφαλή, and that the meaning 'ruler, authority over' has sufficient attestation to establish it clearly as a legitimate sense for κεφαλή in Greek literature at the time of the New Testament.[72]

In addition, he notes that his "findings cover all the meanings mentioned in the major lexicons" that focus on the New Testament period.[73]

Paul's use of headship in 1 Corinthians 11:3 does not allow for equality of roles in marriage. Since creation, God has given the husband authority over the wife. But his authority is to be used in the context of sacrificial love (Eph. 5:25), following the model of the church's subjection to Christ. The headship of a husband over his wife is Paul's main argument in challenging wives not to discard the cultural symbol of their submissiveness to their husbands when they prophesy or pray in a church setting. Such an act would bring disgrace to her husband (v. 5).

The equality between a husband and wife is based on their position in Jesus Christ as part of His body (Gal. 3:28). There is no inferiority implied here. The distinction is in the role or function, not the substance or person.

Headship and equality as joint heirs in Christ are not mutually exclusive. Children who come to Christ are equal in position with their parents, but this does not nullify the commands of Scripture for children to obey their parents. A woman's freedom in Christ does not affect the order of headship in the family that was established at creation. Headship transcends the law and the church. Freedom in Christ does not supersede the hierarchy within the family or the church.

In this passage, Paul logically supports the custom of head coverings for wives based on headship (v. 3), culture (vv. 5, 6), creation (vv. 8, 9), angels (v. 10), nature (v. 14), and church custom (v. 16). The Corinthian women may have rejected the concept of subordination, arguing for their equality because of their freedom from the Mosaic Law and their oneness in Christ. Paul discusses the veiling of wives as a cultural manifestation of submission. He challenges women not to assume that their freedom in Christ is justification for rejecting their cultural expression of submission when they pray and prophesy.

The public head covering was a custom in the first century in both the Jewish and Greco-Roman cultures.[74] Typically, a portion of the outer garment was pulled over the hair like a hood.[75] For a Jewish woman to appear outside of the house with an uncovered head would not only disgrace her husband (*her head* in verse 5), but it was considered shameful (v. 6). MacArthur explains that "Disgraces her head could refer to her own head literally and to her husband's metaphorically."[76] In that day only a prostitute or an extreme feminist would shave her head.[77]

In this passage, Paul emphasizes a distinction in male and female appearance in church services. Kroeger comments:

> This becomes comprehensible when one understands the importance of sex reversal or exchange of sex roles in many ancient religions. Clothing exchange was quite widespread in Dionysiac religion. Corinth was a major center of the cult. At certain religious events women shaved their heads, and men assumed veils or long, flowing hair and golden hairnets.[78]

The New Manners and Customs of Bible Times describes the customs of women during the time of writing this epistle:

> Respectable women went out with their heads covered and wore veils. Only prostitutes displayed their faces and showed off their hair to attract men. Paul therefore tells the Christians that if a woman in the church will not wear a veil, then she should be shorn; but it is best that her head be covered. Even when Christians have liberty in the practice of their faith, they are not to shock propriety.[79]

In Corinth, a woman without a head covering was equated with a prostitute. Also, a Jewish woman who had been convicted of adultery had her head shaved. However,

Greek women removed their head coverings when worshipping in a pagan temple, claiming they belonged to God. In this passage, Paul is explaining that if a woman discarded her head covering, it "was an act not of liberation but of degradation."[80]

As the glory of her husband (v. 7), the wife was not to forsake her complementary role, the cultural expression of which was a head covering. The removal of her head covering, whether as an act of rebellion or a misinterpretation of doctrine, brought dishonor to both her and her head, who was her husband. Waltke summarizes, "Thus women may pray and give expression to the Spirit, but to preserve the Creator's ordering of social relationships they must wear a sign of their subordination."[81]

Clark gives two reasons for the use of head coverings in his commentary on 1 Corinthians.

> The only difference marked by the apostle was, the man had his head uncovered, because he was the representative of Christ; the woman had hers covered, because she was placed by the order of God in a state of subjection to the man, and because it was a custom, both among the Greeks and Romans, and among the Jews an express law, that no woman should be seen abroad without a veil. This was, and is, a common custom through all the east, and none but public prostitutes go without veils. And if a woman should appear in public without a veil,

she would dishonor her head--her husband. And she must appear like to those women who had their hair shorn off as the punishment of whoredom, or adultery.[82]

The Christian Bible Reference Site summarizes the issue of headdressings for worship.

For a Corinthian woman to remove her veil in public would have been an insult to her husband and an affront to the Greek/Roman society in which she lived. Paul strongly discouraged any such rebellion or hint of scandal within the churches. In addition, some pagan priestesses removed their veils and wore their hair disheveled when prophesying. Thus, women should remain veiled while praying or prophesying to avoid any association with paganism.[83]

In verse 10, Paul also uses the argument of angels as spectators in the church (1 Cor. 4:9; Eph. 3:10; 1 Tim. 5:21; cf. Ps. 103:20-21). Since Paul's mention of angels (v.10) as observers of the church (cf. Eph. 3:10) immediately follows the section on creation, it is likely that this correlates with the angels who were present at creation (Job 38:7).[84] These angels observed the creation of Adam and Eve and were aware of the authority that had been given to Adam. Zuck explains:

The angels would be shocked not because they are the guardians of creation, but simply because they have knowledge of the order of creation and what it involves (Job 38:7).

The issue as far as the angels were concerned was whether the Corinthian wives in the church would adhere to God's plan for them, which began at creation and was still in effect.

As is typical of Paul in passages addressing women's issues, in verse 11 the Apostle reminds men that there is interdependence between men and women in the Lord (cf. 1 Pet. 3:7). Reminding them that they are born of women, Paul seems to counteract any potential arrogance on the part of husbands that might come from their knowledge of the doctrine of headship. Submission does not imply inferiority. Both men and women originate from God (v. 12).

In verse 13, Paul appeals to the women to decide for themselves regarding the issue of wearing head coverings. He does not command the wives to wear head coverings, but he tells them to judge for themselves (v. 13) based on the logical arguments of the passage. He assumes that they know it is improper for wives to pray with their heads uncovered.

Having argued culturally and doctrinally for the wearing of head coverings, the Apostle then refers to natural distinctions between men and women in the length of their hair (v. 14). Assuming an affirmative answer, Paul then asks if a woman's long hair is a glory to her (v. 15). Some have taken this verse to mean that long hair is a substitute for a head covering. However, if this were the case, why then does Paul spend this entire passage attempting to convince wives to wear head coverings? Why not just tell them to let their hair grow? Rather, Paul is here referring to femininity as an added distinction between men and women, which would not be affected by their freedom in Christ.

Does not even nature itself teach you that if a man has long hair, it is a dishonor to him, but if a woman has long hair, it is a glory to her? For her hair is given to her for a covering (1 Cor. 11:14–15).

A study note in the NET Bible states: "Paul does not mean nature in the sense of 'the natural world' or 'Mother Nature.' It denotes the 'way things are' because of God's design."[85]

In verse 15, the word *covering* is a different Greek word for head covering than the one used in earlier verses. Commenting on this verse in his commentary, Waltke explains:

> When Paul says that a woman's hair 'is given her for (ajntiv) a covering,' he cannot mean 'in place of' a covering, but rather 'asking for' a covering. Although the Greek preposition frequently implies substitution, that is not its sense here, for such a meaning would render the rest of the argument, especially that in verses 5-6, nonsensical.[86]

Lowery argues that the issue here is a difference between men and women, "Mankind instinctively distinguished between the sexes in various ways, one of which was length of hair." He adds that, "No abstract length of hair was in mind so much as male and female differentiation."[87] The standard for long hair could vary with the culture. The distinction between males and females is clarified in Deuteronomy 22:5, *A woman shall not wear man's clothing, nor shall a man put on a woman's clothing; for whoever does these things is an abomination to the Lord your God.*

Paul next addresses the issue of women who are rebellious or argumentative. He reminds them that none of the other churches have abandoned the use of head coverings (v. 16). The customs of other churches revealed conformity to God's plan. This is Paul's final argument in his attempt to persuade the wives of Corinth to wear head coverings.

The issue in this passage is headship and submission, not head coverings. Eve didn't wear one; neither do the angels. But there is to be a distinction between single and married women. In Corinth, that distinction was a head covering. Paul did not encourage believers to break social custom or status (1 Cor. 7:20). Therefore, the cultural expression of headship by women who prayed and prophesied in the worship assembly was not to be abandoned in favor of freedom in Christ. In fact, verse 10 may be taken that the head covering was a symbol of the woman's equal authority or right to worship God, while being evidence of her functional subordination.

The issue of a head covering was not a moral or religious issue, but a custom. It was not necessarily a matter of the woman's spiritual relationship with God. The passage never states that God will not hear the prayers of women whose heads are not covered. God looks on our hearts, but people look on the outward appearance (1 Sam. 16:7).

There are so many interpretations and applications of this passage, it is difficult to include them all. It seems that those commenting on the use of head coverings are often influenced by their upbringing in various churches. Melick suggests the continuation of the culture of head covering from the time of Paul's writing of the chapter,

> In a carefully reasoned argument, Paul expressed a theological conviction. If a married woman will not proudly wear a symbol of her right relationship to her husband, her familial 'head,' she forfeits her privileges of praying and prophesying in church fellowships. Her ministry in the church is directly linked to her submission to her husband. Paul's words are forceful. Married women have no right to participate in the church service if they wish to assume the prerogative of family headship and/ or if they wish to act as though they were single rather than married. Here proper family order is a prerequisite to a woman's participation in the church.[88]

Wilson agrees, stating, "To be obedient to this passage Christian women should not dress in a way that blurs the distinction between male and female."[89]

In order to apply this passage today, we must first determine the historical setting (cultural practice at the time of writing) and the theological truth (timeless biblical principle) of the text. Instead of attempting to legalistically duplicate the cultural practice of the Corinthian women, we need to recognize the biblical principle of submission to apply this passage to our lives as Christian women today. We must identify the doctrine that applies to every era.

In addition, it is important to evaluate the six factors that Paul used to logically persuade the Corinthian wives to wear head coverings. To apply this passage today in the church, we must determine which factors represent absolute theological truth and which ones refer to the relative historical or cultural practices.

In discussing the origin of this teaching, House summarizes,

> Paul did not base his teaching on mere opinion or rabbinic bias. Rather he clearly founded his teaching on the creation order, the function of the church, and the uniform practice of the church throughout the Roman Empire, in whom also dwelt the Spirit, and obviously the Spirit's leading.[90]

This is an important distinction because the absolute doctrinal issues do not change over time and are valid today. On the other hand, the relative issues that were culturally significant at the time of writing may have changed over the centuries. Therefore, the relative issues must be evaluated in light of each woman's church and social culture. The manner in which a Christian wife manifests her culture's symbol of submission will have an impact on both believers and unbelievers. *"But if one is inclined to be contentious, we have no other practice, nor have the churches of God."* (1 Cor. 11:16)

The biblical principles for determining God's will are important in evaluating relative issues in our lives. In discerning God's will for each of us as individual women today, we must ask ourselves four questions regarding the use or non-use of head coverings in a particular setting. These questions should also be used in any situation where a decision must be made in areas that are not specifically addressed in the Scriptures.

1. Will my participation in it glorify God (1 Cor. 10:31; Col. 3:17)?
2. Will it encourage the spiritual growth of weaker believers (1 Cor. 8:7-13; Heb. 10:24; 2 Pet. 3:18)?
3. Will it win a hearing for the gospel (1 Cor. 9:19-23)?
4. Will it help me grow spiritually (1 Cor. 9:24-27; 10:12; Phil. 1:12; 2 Pet. 3:10)?

The use of non-cultural head coverings today can create a false issue for believer and unbeliever alike. For the believer, it can be assumed to be a sign of holiness, and for the unbeliever it is often a stumbling block to the gospel and true worship. Christian women today must be challenged by this passage to maintain the order of creation and adhere to an expression of their submission and femininity that is appropriate to their culture.

6

Silence in The Church

1 Corinthians 14:34-35

The women should be silent in the churches, for they are not permitted to speak. Rather, let them be in submission, as in fact the law says. If they want to find out about something, they should ask their husbands at home, for it is disgraceful for a woman to speak in church.

This passage appears to be a contradiction of 1 Corinthians 11:5, where women are praying and prophesying. But in 1 Corinthians 14:34, they are commanded to keep silent. Some attempt to resolve this conflict by claiming that the 1 Corinthians 14 passage is a small group meeting, not a church worship service. Others believe that the passage is culturally conditioned. Some state that Paul is not condoning the praying and prophesying of women in 1 Corinthians 14:34, claiming that in fact he disallows it. Others view praying and prophesying as distinct from speaking and teaching. But what does the context of the passage teach us about women being silent in church?

In 1 Corinthians 14, Paul discusses the proper use of spiritual gifts in public assemblies to avoid confusion. His goal is that believers would be unified in their use of a diversity of gifts, stating that the misuse of spiritual gifts causes division and disharmony (1 Cor. 14:4-11, 14-20). He uses the term "keep silent" to provide guidelines for those taking part in a church worship service.

The word *silent* means, "to keep quiet"[91] or "be still."[92] The meaning is more related to ceasing to talk, rather than never speaking or always being quiet.[93] In Luke 18:35-39, the same word is used by the leaders of the multitude to silence a blind man, who was calling out to Jesus, begging for His mercy.

The word *silent* occurs three times in this chapter. Only one of those occurrences refers to women. First, those speaking in tongues without an interpreter are told to keep silent (v. 28). Then, if someone is prophesying and another receives a revelation, the first is to be silent (v. 30). The intent of these admonitions is that believers would yield to one another, taking turns in their ministry of worship and being sensitive to the leading of the Holy Spirit for the purpose of edification and exhortation (vv. 26, 31).

The goal is that the worship service would be orderly and peaceful, that all things would be done properly (vv. 33, 40). Lowery summarizes, "The church members needed to exercise self-control on occasion, a self-control expressed by silence (vv. 28, 30, 34) in order that the assembly might be characterized by peace."[94]

In verse 34, women are admonished to keep silent. There are differences among scholars regarding the reason behind Paul's request for women to be silent. Most agree that it is not an unconditional deterrence of speaking in an assembly because of Paul's earlier reference to women participating in praying and prophesying. Spiritual gifts are bestowed without regard to gender (1 Cor. 12:11). The silence cannot be absolute or else the women could not have sung, prayed, or prophesied. Nor is this a prohibition against women learning in church, but it emphasizes the need for their subjection.

A study note from the NET Bible clarifies this prohibition, stating that "the silence commanded here seems not to involve the absolute prohibition of a woman addressing the assembly."[95] It is probably a prohibition against disruption or verbal dialog by women, which would put them in a position of usurping a teaching role where men were involved. This would be in marked contrast to the activity of women who worship in pagan cults. Most agree that it refers to insubordination to those in authority in the church.

Although praying or prophesying by women is allowed by the Apostle Paul (1 Cor. 14:5) a woman teaching men is not permitted (cf. 1 Tim. 2:12). Apparently, whatever the exact situation is in the church at Corinth, it likely does not refer to the submission of wives to their husbands. The solution, silence, is applicable to all "the churches" (v. 34). Grudem explains that the word *but* in verse 34 indicates,

> A strong contrast between speaking and being subordinate. Thus, the kind of speaking Paul has in mind is specifically speaking that involves insubordination. Not every type of speech would fit this description, but evaluating prophecies aloud certainly would. It would involve assuming the possession of superior authority in matters of doctrinal or ethical instruction especially when it included criticism of the prophecy.[96]

Women are to subject themselves or be in submission *just as the Law also says*. A woman is not to usurp the authority of a male leader, which would be in violation of Scripture. This prohibition seems to be more than merely the disruption of the worship service by disorderly women. If that were the case, why would Paul have to refer to the Law to support his comment?

Paul documents his instructions for women to "subject themselves" by referring to "the Law" (v. 34). Knight explains that,

It is most likely that Paul by this reference to "the law" has in mind God's law and the same passage in that law as that which he cited in 1 Tim. 2:11 ff. and 1 Cor. 11:1 ff., namely the creation order spoken of in Gen. 2.[97]

Smith also comments on Paul's use of the word *law*, noting that it is,

The basis of his authoritative teaching for the church. Paul was evidently not under the misconception that since we are under grace, we have no more to do with the law, a position which, when taken to the logical extreme, is the heresy termed antinomianism.[98]

The law acknowledges the "distinctive roles of men and women."[99] Paul's appeal to the law reveals that his teaching was supported by the Word of God. Rhodes contends Paul citing "the law shows that his argument for the silence of women in church was *theological* and *universal*, not *sociological* or *cultural*."[100] He further states that, "Paul based his argument for female subordination on the order of creation and the purpose of the woman's creation—not on God's declaration to Eve at the Fall."[101]

There are two factors that imply married women are in view in these verses. First, the use of the word *submission* in verse 34. In the New Testament when it is linked to a woman, it always refers to a wife who,

Was to be subject to her husband (Eph. 5:22; Col. 3:18; Titus 2:5; 1 Pet. 3:1, 5). The second indication is the phrase their own husbands (1 Cor. 14:35), whom the inquisitive women were to consult if they had questions.[102]

Some views restrict this limitation of speaking to the judging prophets. One commentator summarizes,

The immediate context concerns self-control and judging the prophets. The prohibition relates to women not being involved in judging the prophets. Such judging would be an expression of authority over men, which was forbidden.[103]

Grudem further rationalizes that a woman's prohibition of vocally critiquing prophets during a church meeting "would not prevent them from silently evaluating the prophecies in their own minds (in fact, v 29 implies that they should do so)."[104]

The NET Bible explains that a woman speaking during an evaluation of a prophet "would be in violation of the submission to male leadership that the OT calls for (the law, e.g., Gen 2:18)."[105]

The women did seem to have a desire to learn. They were just going about it incorrectly. Paul comments in verse 35, *If they desire to learn anything...* But he goes on to say that a church service was not the place to publicly question or debate with those in authority—perhaps those who prophesied. If this were the case, it would clarify that Paul was referring to submission to leadership rather than to their husbands. Interestingly, since women were allowed to prophesy, then it could have been that women prophets might have been among those whom the women were questioning.

In verse 39, Paul summarizes his view on the use of the spiritual gifts of prophecy and tongues in the service,

Therefore, my brethren, desire earnestly to prophesy, and do not forbid to speak in tongues. But all things must be done properly and in an orderly manner.

Paul's use of *brethren* in the Book of 1 Corinthians refers to both men and women in the church. In chapter fourteen, the brethren are seen actively involved in ministry. Therefore, the admonition to wives to keep silent must involve something other than ministry to other believers—most likely it was a failure to submit to male leadership.

It is important to note that the purpose of this passage is peace and order in the church service. For women, the goal was to do that which was proper rather than disgraceful. The relationship between a wife and her husband is not the issue.

Christ: The Model for Marriage

Ephesians 5:22-25

Wives, be subject to your own husbands, as to the Lord. For the husband is the head of the wife, as Christ also is the head of the church, He Himself being the Savior of the body. But as the church is subject to Christ, so also the wives ought to be to their husbands in everything. Husbands, love your wives, just as Christ also loved the church and gave Himself up for her.

The battle of the sexes began in the Garden of Eden. Adam and Eve's sin resulted in a corruption of their God-given roles. But sin did not eliminate these roles. Nor did it create new roles. It was not the initiation of the headship of man. Neither did it cause the prolonging of the roles assumed in the fall—Eve as dominant and Adam as passive. Rather their sin caused a distortion of the roles, which resulted in a power struggle. Only through the power of the Holy Spirit can the outcome of the fall be reversed, and harmony be restored between a husband and wife.

Ephesians 5:22-33 challenges wives to submit to their husbands with respect and husbands to love their wives with the same sacrificial, unselfish love as Christ loves the church. In this passage, Paul refers to men as the head of the marriage relationship. He also repeats this command in Colossians 3:18, *Wives, submit to your own husbands, as is fitting in the Lord.* The Greek word, *hupotasso*, which is translated *submit, subject,* or *obey* is "primarily a military term, meaning 'to rank under.'"[106] It does not imply either slavery or inferiority.

Shirley Taylor disagrees, arguing that "Male headship is a flawed theology that perpetuates violence against women." She argues, "The only way the church can make it unacceptable to beat, kill, or maim women and children, is to stop teaching the flawed theology of male headship."[107]

But this is like claiming that child abuse is the result of children being under their parents' authority. Abuse is not caused by the biblical role of the abusers, but by sin in their lives resulting from a failure to fulfil their God-given role by being led by the Holy Spirit. A desire for control is evidence of a refusal to yield to the Lord and trust Him. Abuse can be by a parent, a husband, or a wife. The Freedom for Christian Women Coalition asserted that the submission of a wife "'is more about power and control than about love or obeying the Word of God." It challenged the Council on Biblical Manhood and Womanhood to condemn the Danvers Statement and to acknowledge the harm it has done to churches and "confess it as sin."[108]

Melick argues that,

> The Greek term used for submission, *hypotasso*, suggests a voluntary submission based on a commitment to proper order. It does not imply an organization based on inability or inferiority. Indeed, this term seems to have been chosen by Paul to honor the unique value of the wife. In a beautiful tension, he affirms both value and order, both equality and subordination.[109]

Submission should not be characterized as being passive, weak, or inferior. A submissive wife is not a slave to be ordered around by her husband. Submission is not blind obedience regardless of what the Bible states about an action.[110] A husband and wife should interact together in unity. They are not to be competitors. "If a house is divided against itself, that house will not be able to stand" (Mark 3:25). The vow of mutual fidelity made by husband and wife is not made exclusively by each one to the other, but by each to God.[111] A Spirit-led submissive wife is cooperative and supportive of a godly husband.

The husband is commanded in Scripture to honor his wife as a fellow heir of God's grace, although her role is weaker. She is not a weaker person. He just has the stronger role. His failure to honor her would result in his prayers not being answered due to his loss of fellowship with God.

> *You husbands in the same way, live with your wives in an understanding way, as with someone weaker, since she is a woman; and show her honor as a fellow heir of the grace of life, so that your prayers will not be hindered* (1 Pet. 3:7).

Dr. Howard Hendricks reacted to one of his students at Dallas Theological Seminary who came to his office one day complaining about his wife. Dr. Hendricks' response was to ask him, "Are you granting her honor?"

Husbands are urged repeatedly to love their wives (Eph. 5:25, 28, 33). Wives are exhorted to respect their husbands (Eph. 5:33) but are not commanded to love them. Yet as Paul exhorts older women to be reverent in their behavior so they *encourage the young women to love their husbands... being subject to their own husbands, so that the word of God will not be dishonored* (Titus 2:3–5). In Ephesians 5, Paul uses the word *agape* for love. But in Titus 2, the wife is encouraged to respond to her husband fondly and affectionately, using the Greek word for philanthropy.

A husband and wife are to be a team—a team created and designed by God—working together to honor the Lord. A team can be stronger and accomplish much more for the Lord as one unit than they ever could as two individuals. A husband-wife team is like a duet. The consequence should be harmony as they uplift and support each other.

The song "Wind Beneath My Wings" wonderfully describes how spouses can enrich and encourage each other. "You did your best to make me shine. You are my hero. I could fly higher than an eagle 'cause you are the wind beneath my wings. I would be nothing without you."[112]

A wife should not try to be like a man or attempt to function in the same way. A wife's purpose is not to duplicate her husband's role or to replace it, but to complement it. She can minister in ways that a man never could. She is feminine; he is not.

They are different people with different talents and spiritual gifts (1 Cor. 12:12, 14-20). They need to communicate and plan together (Eph. 4:32; 1 Cor. 7:5; Phil 2:3). They need to learn to be kind, forgive each other, and not hold grudges (Eph. 4:32; Col. 4:13; 1 John 1:9). They must individually and together commit their way to the Lord (Prov. 3:5, 6). They must be faithful to the Lord and to each other (Gal. 5:22, 23). Hodge explains, "The vow of mutual fidelity made by husband and wife, is not made exclusively by each one to the other, but by each to God."[113] They need to pray together and for each other (Matt. 18:19; 2 Tim. 1:3). Their goal is to grow closer to the Lord (Eph. 4:15; 2 Pet. 3:18. God is to be the center of their relationship. As they grow closer to Him, they will grow closer to each other.

8

The Daughters of Eve

1 Timothy 2:9-15

Likewise the women are to dress in suitable apparel, with modesty and self-control. Their adornment must not be with braided hair and gold or pearls or expensive clothing, but with good deeds, as is proper for women who profess reverence for God. A woman must learn quietly with all submissiveness. But I do not allow a woman to teach or have authority over a man. She must remain quiet. For Adam was formed first and then Eve. And Adam was not deceived, but the woman, because she was fully deceived, fell into transgression. But she will be delivered through childbearing, if she [they] continue[s] in faith and love and holiness with self-control.

The occasion of false teachers in Ephesus prompted Paul to write the First Epistle to Timothy, which is considered one his pastoral epistles. Paul spent two years in Ephesus, a political, religious, and commercial center. The temple of the Greek goddess Artemis in Ephesus was one of the Seven Wonders of the World.[114] Timothy was the son of a gentile Greek father and a Jewish mother. Upon leaving for Macedonia, Paul urged his beloved co-worker Timothy to remain in Ephesus so that he could "instruct certain men not to teach strange doctrines" (1 Tim. 1:3) as opposed to "sound teaching according to the glorious gospel of the blessed God" (vv. 10, 11).

Timothy had known "the sacred writings" from childhood (2 Tim. 3:15), likely taught to him by his grandmother Lois and his mother Eunice (2 Tim. 1:5). The emphasis on the importance of the Word of God in 1 and 2 Timothy is evidenced using fifty-five synonyms for the words *teach* and *doctrine*. This is clearly noted in 1 Timothy 3:16-17:

All Scripture is inspired by God and profitable for teaching, for reproof, for correction, for training in righteousness; that the man of God may be adequate, equipped for every good work.

The epistle of First Timothy includes directives for proper conduct in the worship assembly that included both men and women (1 Tim 1:3-11; 4:1-5). In the context of a church worship service in chapter two, the Apostle Paul exhorts believers to godliness in contrast to wrath and dissension by the men, and in place of rebellion and lack of submissiveness on the part of the women. Although the Greek words for *men* and *women* could also be translated *husbands* and *wives*, this is unlikely due to the content of the entire passage.

Paul encourages the manifestation of godliness in the life of women in the church. Instead of behaving in a godly way, the lavish dress and actions of some women were symbolic of either a lack of sensitivity or perhaps even rebellion.

In light of the importance of Ephesus as a commercial center, it is also possible that these were wealthy women who could have been proudly displaying their expensive attire or perhaps they were merely dressing in their best clothes to honor their newfound God as they worshipped Him. In either case, the apparel of women was apparently distracting worshippers. Freedom in Christ may have been an issue here as well as in 1 Corinthians 11. This is not a prohibition against makeup or accessories, but a matter of priorities (1 Pet. 3:3; Eze. 16:10).

The Apostle Paul admonishes Christian women to dress modestly with decency and the absence of sexual suggestiveness (cf. the adulterous woman of Proverbs 7:10-11), having an appearance that is simple, moderate, and sensible), and free from ostentation (showiness). In other words, Paul is telling the women not to dress like pagan women who are trying to attract attention to themselves (Pro. 7:10-11).

Women are to dress in a manner that reflects inner purity and is appropriate for worship. Paul's instruction to these women might be likened to Proverbs 11:22, *As a ring of gold in a swine's snout, So is a beautiful woman who lacks discretion.*

This proverb is a bit humorous to us as we read it today. But in the Jewish culture, this is a linking of the most valuable item in their society (gold) with that which they considered to be the vilest (swine). This combination would have been shameful to the Jewish people. They clearly understood the impossibility of uniting these two things. The women in particular would have known how distasteful a lack of discretion could be.

Paul is telling the Ephesian women that their claim to godliness must be apparent in the way they dress. They should be known for the good deeds they perform, not for how they look. The contrast here is between a woman who walks into church dressed to call attention to herself, and one who is occupied with her worship of God and the performance of good works. The latter focuses on the Lord and is thinking of others rather than herself. Christian women must be discerning and discreet in their choice of clothes. Also, husbands and fathers need to discourage the immodest attire of their wives and daughters, especially in the context of church worship.

In verse 11, Paul states that in contrast to an outward manifestation of rebellion and selfishness, women should be teachable, with an attitude of submissiveness, learning quietly (not disrupting or domineering). Paul is actually elevating the status of women in this verse. Learning in quietness places the instruction of women in line with that of rabbinic students, thereby emphasizing both the equality of women and the seriousness of learning. Quietness in this passage, rather than being a rebuke, is a condition of learning that reveals the heart attitude of women—that their teachers are worthy of respect. Quietness is a state of undisturbed calmness, which enables one to learn. It does not denote complete silence (Luke 18:39; 1 Cor. 14:34). Rather it means, "settled down, undisturbed, not unruly" (Acts 22:2; 2 Thes. 3:12).[115]

The submission in this verse is not that of a wife to her husband but is an attitude of submission to the teacher with the expectation that the listener would accept the teaching. This verse clearly teaches that women are to learn the Word of God.

Verse twelve has become one of the most frequently debated verses among those with differing opinions regarding the issue of women teaching men in the church. A plethora of books and journal articles have been written on this subject. There are many differing opinions, interpretations, and applications. In response to a question about women as pastors, GotQuestions.com comments, "This is not an issue of chauvinism or discrimination. It is an issue of biblical interpretation.[116]

Some have argued that the phrase, "But I do not allow," shows that this was Paul's personal opinion and does not reflect the direct will of God on this issue. However, in this same chapter, Paul uses the phrases, "I urge" and "I want" when making requests of believers. In 1 Timothy 2:1, Paul says, "I urge that entreaties and prayers, petitions and thanksgivings, be made on behalf of all men." Then verse 7, he states, "I want the men in every place to pray, lifting up holy hands, without wrath and dissension."

If we take the prohibition of women teaching men to be Paul's judgment for a church plagued with false preachers, then should we also disregard his admonition to pray for those in authority or to pray without dissension?

It has also been suggested that, due to the use of the present indicative use of *permit*, this verse was limited in its scope—only referring to the time of destination of the epistle, rather than having a universal and timeless appeal. Knight explains:

> An examination of other occurrences of Paul's use of first person singular present indicative (Rom. 12:1, 3; 1 Cor. 4:16; 2 Cor. 5:20; Gal. 5:2, 3; Eph. 4:1; 1 Thes. 4:1; 5:14; 2 Thes. 3:6; 1 Tim. 2:1, 8) demonstrates that he uses it to give universal and authoritative instruction or exhortation (cf. especially Rom. 12:1; 1 Tim. 2:8).[117]

Some women seek to justify the fact that they are pastoring a church or teaching men by saying that they have been anointed or called by God. The issue is that God would not call someone to do something that is contrary to His Word. Would God call someone to do that which He forbids in Scripture? When there is a conflict between personal calling and the Word of God, the Scripture must take preeminence. Here again, the issue of inerrancy and authority of Scripture must be honored. The answer is found in the Word of God, not in someone's experience.

Many years ago, when commenting on 1 Timothy 2:12, one well-known woman pastor in Los Angeles said, "That is where Paul and I disagree." In other words, she was placing herself in authority over the Apostle Paul and the inspiration of the Word of God. Feminists often characterize Paul as one who hates women. But rather than presenting a biased view, Paul is merely restating God's plan for women throughout the ages.

In verse 12, Paul's injunction for women not to *teach or exercise authority over a man* contrasts with his encouragement for them to learn the Word of God. In the early church, teaching was based on the Jewish model. Teaching involved more than merely the transmitting of information. Teachers were typically leaders in the community or masters who had disciples. The authority of the teacher was grounded in a trusting relationship between the teacher and his students or disciples.[118]

Teaching in the Pastoral Epistles included judging, reproving, exhortation, and rebuke (2 Tim. 4:1-4). The teacher was to speak confidently, shun controversy, and reject divisive persons (Titus 3:8-11), speaking, exhorting, and approving with all authority (Tit. 2:15). House explained:

> If false teaching per se were Paul's concern in 2:8-15, certainly he would have also prohibited men from such teaching. But the emphasis is not on women teaching false doctrines, but on women teaching men.[119]

If women would teach in the context of church worship, they would be placing themselves in authority over men (including their own husbands). They would also be usurping the teaching ministry of the elder (1 Tim. 3:2), whose ministry is to take care of or manage the church.[120]

In response to the question asking what the Bible says about women pastors, GodQuestions.com, replies:

> The city of Ephesus was known for its temple to Artemis, a false Greek/Roman goddess. Women were the authority in the worship of Artemis. However, the book of 1 Timothy nowhere mentions Artemis, nor does Paul mention Artemis worship as a reason for the restrictions in 1 Timothy 2:11-12.[121]

An elder must have a skillful ability to instruct or teach, with a goal of not only instructing believers, but refuting false teaching with sound doctrine. The ability to teach does not qualify one to teach in the context of a worship service. Women may have the spiritual gift of teaching, but they must not use that gift in a setting that is prohibited in Scripture.

The women are to remain quiet in contrast to teaching or being in authority over men. The word quiet "describes an attitude of peaceable acceptance and is different from the word translated *silent* in 1 Corinthians 14:34."[122]

This corrective measure was probably taken by Paul to offset the behavior of women who were abusing their freedom in Christ or misapplying their equality in the Body of Christ. Teaching privately or teaching other women was not only permitted, but also encouraged (Acts 18:26; Titus 2:3-4). The issue in verse 12 is women being in the position of authority over men in the church. Paul is not prohibiting women from teaching but is restricting the sphere of their gift not to include teaching men. This is not an issue of spiritual gifts. Some believers, women as well as men, have been given the gift of teaching.

There are many venues in which women can teach—conferences, the Internet, radio, music, poetry, books, etc. But they are responsible to God to accurately interpret the Scriptures. Perhaps the greatest opportunity God has given women is to teach children. Training children to be godly adults is one of the greatest needs in Christianity today. Women are not to pastor men, but they have the wonderful privilege of teaching young boys, and teens to become godly men. This is one of the greatest ministries of the church and the home.

If the issue were only false teaching, then why bring up authority. This is not an injunction against a woman teaching her husband. There is nothing in Scripture that prohibits a husband from learning from his wife. Remember the context here is the church service. This is a pastoral epistle, along with 2 Timothy and Titus, that is designed to address doctrinal issues and church government. Knight explains:

> That which is prohibited is teaching (didaskein) and having dominion (*authentein*).14 The prohibition is not absolute or unqualified, but it is specifically that she as a woman must not engage in such activities in relation to a man (*andros*). The prohibition is not that a woman may not teach anyone (cf. Titus 2:3, 4) but that she must not teach and have authority over a man in the life of the church.[123]

A view that some women hold today is that women can teach men or preach in the pulpit if the pastor or elders of the church give them the authority. They believe that the command here only forbids them to usurp authority. They conclude that if the authority is given to them, then it is permissible for them to preach and teach. However, this passage does not support this view. Teaching and authority are separate issues. Paul did not say women are not to teach authoritatively. Instead of teaching men or having authority over them, women are instructed to remain quiet. How can one who obeys this command of Paul teach men, even with the permission of male leaders in the church, if she is to remain quiet?

Some use Priscilla as an example of women teaching men in the New Testament. However, the word *teach* is not used in Acts 18:26, where Priscilla, along with her husband Aquila, explain doctrine to Apollos. It is important to note that this was done privately and in a team ministry with her husband. In addition, some proponents of women teaching men refer to the fact that the women at the tomb were commissioned by the risen Christ to declare the news of the resurrection to the disciples (Matt. 28:10). Neither of these two instances can be used as examples of women teaching men. Both these passages are narratives and cannot be considered normative for the New Testament church. Neither of them occurred in a church setting. Women are not forbidden to teach or influence men privately, but they must be careful to do it in a godly manner with an accurate interpretation of Scripture.

Some teach that the reason for Paul's refusal to allow women to teach men was because false teachers had deceived them. This view argues that the command is limited to the time of writing, thereby permitting women today to be pastors, Sunday school teachers, and church board members. However, the culture at the time of writing cannot affect the interpretation in a manner that would be inconsistent with other Scripture.[124]

Women are to be known for their good works and for their submission to those teaching the Word of God.

However, they are not permitted to teach or exercise authority over men in the church. If the influence of false teachers were the only problem, then learning correct doctrine would then allow them to teach. It seems unlikely that women would have been the only ones who would have been unfavorably influenced by false teachers. Men would also have been likely to communicate false doctrine when they taught. The presence of false teachers cannot be used as proof for the prohibition of women teaching men. If false teachers were the only reason for women not to teach men, then neither should they teach men today because there are still false teachers in the churches. False teaching provided the context for the prohibition, but the order of creation provided the reason.

In verses 13-15, Paul refers to creation, the fall, and the curse as an explanation for his prohibition. In Verse 13, the word *for* or *because* is used, showing the reason for Paul's previous statement. Paul clearly explains that the basis of his restriction is the order of creation. The reason women are not to teach or exercise authority over men is not because of false teachers, but because Adam was created first.

Some have assumed that Paul is teaching that women are more easily deceived than men. But this view is denied by Paul in his warning to the church, *But I fear, lest somehow, as the serpent deceived Eve by his craftiness, so your minds may be corrupted from the simplicity that is in Christ* (2 Cor. 11:3).

Eve's deception was due to the situation and circumstances of her temptation, not a weakness in her character. But she was not solely responsible for sin entering the world. Adam's authority caused him to receive the blame. Romans 5:12 states, *Therefore, just as through one man sin entered into the world, and death through sin, and so death spread to all men, because all sinned.*

Adam was punished for accepting Eve's offer to eat of the fruit of the tree of life —a clear indication of her forsaking her role. This is exactly what was happening in Ephesus. Women were being deceived into thinking they could teach men, ignoring the creative order.

Paul then refers to the fact that it was Eve, not Adam who was deceived. In the context of this passage, the emphasis is on the fact that Eve was deceived into abandoning her God-given role. This is precisely what Paul is warning women against in the Ephesian church.

Verse 15 has been interpreted in various ways and is considered by some to be one of the most difficult verses in the New Testament to understand. The phrase preserved through the bearing of children has been understood as: 1) physical safety in childbirth, 2) salvation through the birth of Christ, or 3) deliverance from insignificance in the church and corruption in society through motherhood.

However, in the Greek, the verb "preserved" is singular and refers back to Eve in verse 13. But the word *continue* is in the plural referring to "children." The verse should read:

She [Eve] shall be saved through childbearing if they [women who are the offspring of Eve] abide in faith and love and sanctification with self-control.

Christian women today are to fulfill the role that God designed for Eve. We are to be what she should have been. When we (as Eve's children) pursue godliness with self-restraint and are not deceived, Eve (through us) is restored to her rightful place. Such women prove to the church and to the world that godly women can fulfill their original God-given role to the glory of God.

Although women are equal with men in their position in Christ, we learn from this passage that equality in position is not equality in role. A Christian woman is prohibited from teaching and exercising leadership over men in the local church, but she can minister to others using her spiritual gifts and by her godly example. Older women are exhorted to encourage younger women (Titus 2:3) and to teach children (2 Tim. 1:5; 3:14-15).

Woman to Woman

Titus 2:3-5

Older women likewise are to exhibit behavior fitting for those who are holy, not slandering, not slaves to excessive drinking, but teaching what is good. In this way they will train the younger women to love their husbands, to love their children, to be self-controlled, pure, fulfilling their duties at home, kind, being subject to their own husbands, so that the message of God may not be discredited.

Since this passage is often referenced as the primary text for women's ministry, many questions have arisen regarding its interpretation. Who are the older women? What does it mean for them to be reverent in their behavior? Are the subjects which women are permitted to teach limited to the specific topics listed in the passage regarding young women?

The theme of Titus is found in its first verse: *knowledge of the truth which leads to godliness* (1:1). The Apostle Paul, a bondservant of God, desired that the faith of God's chosen people would result in knowledge of the Scriptures that produced godly living.

The purpose of Paul's epistle to Titus was to instruct him regarding his teaching and administration in the churches on the island of Crete in Greece. Titus was directed to set things in order and appoint qualified elders in every city (1:5-9). Historically, the Cretans to whom Titus ministered were disgracefully immoral (1:10-16). The rebellious and deceptive false teachers claimed to know God intimately, but their actions contradicted them (1:16). Titus was to silence them and reprove them severely in order that their doctrine would be corrected.

On the other hand, Paul exhorted Titus to teach what was in harmony with sound doctrine (2:1). The context for the passage is speaking that which is suitable or fitting for sound doctrine in contrast to false teaching. In addition to the advice that Paul gives to Titus in this chapter, there are specific instructions for five groups of people: older men, older women, young women, young men, and slaves.

After challenging older men to godly living, which is characterized by temperance, dignity, sensibility, soundness in faith, love, and perseverance, Paul turns his focus to older women. The phrase, *older women*, is from the same Greek root as the word *elder* (1:5). It can mean "an adult female advanced in years," but when used in the context with young women is more of a term of comparison.[125] While Paul gives Titus instructions regarding both the older and younger men, it is the older women who are to minister to the young women. Of course, the women would learn during the worship time or Bible studies, but their one-on-one discipleship was to be woman-to-woman. This is important for two reasons. First, older women can encourage young women in areas that they have personal experience. Only another woman can counsel a woman regarding what it is like to be a wife and mother. In addition, this would also help prevent lack of discretion on the part of Titus and other male leaders.

The Greek phrase, *reverent behavior*, does not occur elsewhere in the New Testament. The word *reverent* is derived from the same root as *holy* and means, "suited to sacred character, consecrated in behavior." The word *behavior*, which means, "conduct with a focus on demeanor or attitude," is defined in the context as well as in secular literature. It is a complex term that includes attitudes, actions, attire, and speech. The significance of the term reverent in behavior is that older women are admonished to act godly, like women who have been redeemed and made saints. In contrast to the false teachers in Crete whose lives did not concur with their profession to know God, these women were to live in such a way that no one would doubt that they were believers.

The phrase, *likewise are to be reverent in their behavior*, equates the lifestyle of the older women to that of the older men in the previous verse. In other words, reverent behavior is temperate, dignified, sensible, sound in faith, loving, and persevering. A life that is reverently consistent with sound doctrine then becomes the basis for qualifying these older women for ministry to young women. The next two descriptions are stated in the negative. These are things that the women were to avoid in their lives. Their presence would prohibit reverent behavior. The older women are not to falsely accuse others. The word *slanderous*, in the noun form is a title for the Devil (1 Pet. 5:8).[126] It means that the older women were not to falsely accuse someone or speak critically with the intention of hurting another person (cf. 1 Tim 3:11), they were not to be addicted or enslaved to wine (cf. 1 Tim. 3:8).

In 1 Timothy 5:11-13, Paul denounces the young widows, probably those who were childless. They had become idle, that is, useless or unproductive, going around from house to house and being gossips (babbling and talking foolishly) and busybodies (curious, paying attention to things which do not concern them). Older women would also be tempted to misuse their free time, which could be better spent ministering to young women.

In contrast to the false teachers in Crete (2 Pet. 2:1), the older women were to teach that which was intrinsically good. The term, *teachers of good*, occurring only here in the New Testament, means "one who teaches what is good and morally right" as opposed to that which is false. The term is used in a "pastoral or ethical sense," implying a relationship between the teacher and her pupil. The purpose is also to teach theoretical and practical knowledge with the highest level of the development of the pupil. Godliness is to be modeled by the older women as an essential condition for teaching.

The older women were to be the opposite of the disorderly, empty talkers, and deceivers of Titus 1:10 who led people astray. *Teachers of what is good* would mean that their lives and words would be in harmony with the Word of God. The term "teachers of good" is a title, implying that this is like a profession. They were "official teachers." It is similar to the phrase that was common in Israel, "teachers of the law" (Luke 5:17; Acts 5:34). The only other title given to teachers in the New Testament is that which describes the rebellious men mentioned in chapter one, "teachers of evil," or false teachers (2 Pet. 2:1).

There is an emphasis in the Epistle to Titus on fruitfulness or good works of believers, which has sound doctrine as its basis (1:16; 2:7, 14; 3:8, and 14). Titus 2:4 begins with a purpose clause, indicating the intent of the qualifications for the older women that are specified in verse 3. The word *train* means to "instruct someone to behave in a wise and becoming manner." The older women were to be godly for the purpose of encouraging, advising, or urging young women.[127]

In summary, Paul is saying that now that the older women are empty nesters, they need to act in a godly way so they will be qualified to minister to young women. The lifestyle of the older women should create both an interest in and a thirst for godliness on the part of the young women. The result is that the young women would be teachable in terms of improving both their character and their actions.

Who are these young women that are to be trained? If they were the daughters of these women, would Paul not have labeled them as such? Perhaps they were young women who were new believers who did not have Christian mothers. They would not be aware of the teaching of the Scriptures regarding godliness and Christlike relationships within a family. They were to be encouraged to love their husbands and children, treating them with kindness and affection. The focus here is not on a love that is from the heart, but a love that is manifest in gracious actions to others rather than an angry critical spirit. The Greek word, *phileo*, focuses on interpersonal affection in a relationship while *agape* stresses love and affection based on deep appreciation and high regard. Both terms are used of the relations between the Father and the Son and between God and believers (John 3:35; 5:20; 16:27; Rom. 8:28). The young women were to create an attitude of kindness and acceptance in the home.

When my husband was a youth pastor, the mother of three of the youth died of cancer. The older son made a comment to us that I have never forgotten. He said that when a father dies, the family loses its head and provider. But when a family loses the mother, it loses the heartbeat of the home.

As the heartbeat of the family, the role of the mother is vital, acting as an adhesive that holds the family together.

The older women were also to urge the young women to behave in a sensible or wise manner, in other words, to have self-control. They were also to admonish them to be morally pure, free from defilement or contamination (1 John 3:2-3). Their primary focus in life was to be their home, which they were to take care of and manage. Their example was Proverbs 31, a portrait of a godly woman who manages her home, honors her husband, cares for her children, and fears the Lord. The young women were to be workers at home, perhaps in contrast to idle women who went from home-to-home gossiping and meddling.

There are two different stages of life represented here. The older woman has already raised her children and now has time to minister. But the younger woman is busily involved in the daily tasks of a young wife and mother. Paul is exhorting the older women to build a ministry, but he is admonishing the younger women to build a home. Only then, like the elders of 1 Timothy 3:4, will they be qualified to do the work of the ministry. Chuck Swindoll comments, "There is no more influential or powerful role on earth than a mother's."[128]

The New Testament is practically silent on childrearing. The Book of Proverbs was the textbook of the home in Old Testament times and its timeless, practical principles continue to be of value today. The Hebrew home was the incubator of Jewish virtues and the perpetuator of the teachings of the Torah. The value of a Christian home today is not limited to its family members. A godly home is the foundation of a moral society and the perpetuator of Christianity in a nation.

In ancient Jewish families, children were highly esteemed—the hope of Israel's future. The responsibility of parents in child training was the dominant factor in Jewish education. This is illustrated by the Hebrew words for teach, instruct, tell, command, rebuke, restrain, chasten, guide and train, which are frequently used in the Old Testament when admonishing parents.

Every word, deed, and action in the Hebrew life experience was an occasion for child education. *Impress them upon your children. Talk about them when you sit at home and when you walk along the road, when you lie down and when you get up* (Deut. 6:7).

Parental responsibility in childrearing begins at birth and continues to maturity. There is urgency in discipline;[129] it is to begin early before the child forms firm habit patterns. Proverbs 22:6, *Train up a child in the way he should go, even when he is old he will not depart it,* emphasizes the importance of starting a young child off on the right path.

Training children in godliness must begin early in life. If a young mother puts her children in daycare only so she can build a career or earn money to raise her standard of living, she willingly forfeits some of her opportunity to train them in godliness. Her goal in parenting should be to wean children off their parents and onto the Lord and his Word. In this sense, the training never ends; its source merely changes.

The younger women were also to be good and to place themselves under subjection to their own husbands in order that the Word of God would not be blasphemed (spoken of in an evil way) (1 Tim. 6:1). Lives lived in accordance with sound doctrine would be a testimony to the truthfulness of the Scriptures and would win a hearing for the gospel.

Paul's goal in this passage is that the godliness of the older women would qualify them to teach the young women how to be a testimony to the Lord to the unbelievers in Crete. The older women would become more Christlike, the younger women would grow in the Lord through what they are taught by word and example, and the unbelievers of Crete would see that godly living honors the Word of God. The Word of God should influence the way we live as believers.

We have learned from this passage that the ministry of women is needed in the church. Older women with free time are to spend it encouraging young women in the Lord. Godliness is to be modeled by the older women as an essential condition for ministry. They are to encourage the young women, not out of a vacuum, but as an overflow of their personal walk with the Lord. Their lives are to be in harmony with sound doctrine. How is this possible if they do not know the Bible?

A woman needs to know the Scriptures in order to be equipped for "works of service." She can then be a vital instrument in helping to build up the Body of Christ. She is an important part of the church. Her ministry is essential, and it is not limited to encouraging young women. Women can be a dynamic influence on others by their godly example and through the use of their spiritual gifts. They are to be like a magnet that attracts both believers and unbelievers to Christ. What a challenge to women today!

10

The Weaker Vessel

1 Peter 3:1-7

In the same way, wives, be subject to your own husbands. Then even if some are disobedient to the word, they will be won over without a word by the way you live, when they see your pure and reverent conduct. Let your beauty not be external—the braiding of hair and wearing of gold or fine clothes— but the inner person of the heart, the lasting beauty of a gentle and tranquil spirit, which is precious in God's sight. For in the same way the holy women who hoped in God long ago adorned themselves by being subject to their husbands, like Sarah who obeyed Abraham, calling him lord. You become her children when you do what is good and have no fear in doing so. Husbands, in the same way, treat your wives with consideration as the weaker partners and show them honor as fellow heirs of the grace of life. In this way nothing will hinder your prayers.

The biblical model for marriage is found in Ephesians 5:22-33 where the filling of the Holy Spirit in the lives of the husband and wife produces a godly marriage, one of the greatest witnesses for the gospel. The Apostle Paul describes a godly wife as one who submits to her husband, as unto the Lord (Eph. 5:22). A Spirit-filled husband loves his wife as Christ loves the church (Eph. 5:25).

The roles of male and female, authority, and submission, are to be balanced in harmony and unity through the power of the Holy Spirit. The husband and wife, who are equal in their position in Christ, have different functions within the marriage. The roles that were designed by God and inaugurated at the creation of Adam and Eve remain unchanged. This teaching is in direct opposition to the Christian feminists' view that headship began at the fall and ended at the cross.

In the Ephesians passage, Paul is merely restating God's original plan, revealing that its implementation is only possible through the filling of the Spirit. Sinful natures, acquired at the fall, will always be in conflict, creating discord. Only through the filling of the Holy Spirit can there be peace and love in the home. The husband is to combine his God-given authority with sacrificial love. His wife is to submit to his leadership as unto the Lord. The Apostle Peter also applies the submissive role to Christian wives, even if their husbands are unbelievers. The goal is that their husbands would come to Christ.

The First Epistle of Peter is written to Christians who had been scattered throughout the world and were being persecuted as they lived in a pagan and hostile society. In the same way, Peter refers to the examples of submission by citizens to governmental authorities, by slaves to masters, and even by Christ Himself as He endured suffering on our behalf. The subject of the context is unjust persecution.

In this passage, Peter challenges believing wives to adorn themselves with godly submission as a testimony to their husbands, even those who are disobedient to the Word of God, meaning the gospel. By application, this could also include husbands who are believers, but are not walking with the Lord (Eph. 5:22; Col. 3:18). Conversion to Christ did not exempt wives from being under the authority of their husbands who had not come to Christ. God's design from the beginning is that the husband be the head of the home, the wife's newly acquired relationship with Christ did not change God's original plan. Submission is not inferiority; it is a matter of function based on the order of creation. However, it is important to note that this passage does not require women to be submissive to men in general but only to their own husbands. As will be noted, there are limitations to her submission.

Submission does not require that one give up the right of expression or opinion. Submission is not passive. It is the active choice of a godly woman—a voluntary yielding in love (Eph. 5:21; 1 Pet. 5:5). It is an acceptance of the wife's role in the home under the leadership of her husband, whom God has placed as head in the home. It is an attitude of yieldedness to a God-given authority. Headship in the home is not to be shared. It is a God-ordained role, not a choice. Jesus explained in Mark 3:25, "If a house is divided against itself, that house will not be able to stand." The result will be fighting and arguing.

The goal of this passage is that the pagan husband be won to Christ by the behavior of his believing wife. For the unbelieving husband, the object is his salvation; for the disobedient believer, the object is repentance and obedience to the Word. Without a word does not mean that she is not to share the gospel or the Scriptures with her husband. But it is her behavior, not her preaching or criticism, which touches the heart of her unbelieving husband and wins him to the Lord.

The wife's undefiled life, based on her fear of the Lord, is one that shows respect to her husband. Both her behavior and her appearance are to reflect godliness in contrast to the women of the world. Her inner beauty—a gentle and peaceful spirit—is precious in the sight of the Lord. Swindoll explains, "Without question, this is any woman's most powerful quality—true character."[130] It is a manifestation of her trust in the Lord and her acceptance of her femaleness as designed by God. Her most important attraction is her spirituality, not her physical appearance. Such a gentle and quiet spirit is of great value to God.

Peter clarifies the difference between the role or function of the husband and wife as contrasted to their position in Christ. Yet, while there may be equality in personhood and in salvation, there is a hierarchy in roles. By calling upon wives to submit to their husbands (1 Pet 3:1), Peter reveals to the reader where authority resides in marriage, as well as how the marriage relationship is to function. Paul does the same in Ephesians 5:22–33.[131]

Peter then uses Sarah as an example of a submissive wife. Her obedience to Abraham was grounded in her trust in the Lord. Submission requires that wives place the outcome in the Lord's hands, which results in peace rather than fear. However, submission is conditional in doing what is not contrary to the Word of God. To do what is right is to do that which is good or that which is precise in the sense of fulfilling Christian moral law.

In verse 7, the wife is referred to in two ways: 1) a weaker vessel, who should have her husband's understanding (knowledge), and 2) a co-inheritor of the grace of life, requiring that her husband honor and respect her. Popular explanations of the meaning of the term *weaker vessel* include emotional or physical weakness. However, the context of the passage does not support these definitions. Neither does the depiction of Eve's creation in Genesis. There is no evidence that God made her inferior to Adam as some would argue—stating that her being more easily deceived is the reason Satan tempted her rather than Adam. The context of verses 1-6 is a wife's submission to her husband. Therefore, the meaning of weaker vessel must be in relationship to submission. She is weaker in rank. The Apostle does not use the term weaker person but uses *vessel* in a figurative sense.

The view that *vessel* refers to the woman in a physical or emotional sense distorts and limits the biblical use of this word. The interpretation that "weakness in view here is primarily physical weakness, since the term vessel means the human body,"[132] fails to consider the role of the wife within the marriage.

The adjective *weaker*, used with the word *vessel*, is comparative to the unspecified stronger vessel, or her husband. Although some would say both are weak, with she being the weaker vessel. The wife is in a secondary, or weaker, role. But in her relationship to Christ, as a fellow possessor of eternal life, she is equal. The *weaker vessel* is in reference to her function; the phrase *fellow heir* refers to her position in Christ (cf. Gal. 3:28). Youngblood explains, "In an even broader sense, vessel refers to people who carry within them the knowledge of God (2 Cor. 4:6–7).[133]

A wife is to be honored by her husband. This is so important that if he does not honor her, his prayer life will be hindered. She is equal to her husband in created essence and has become equal to him in her position in Christ, but she is unequal in function. Her God-given role is weaker, but it is of great value to the Lord. In His infinite love, God created woman as a counterpart for man. Not to compete, but to complement. Wives are not to replace or dominate their husbands but do what we do best—be a woman! But godliness is our greatest asset.

11

Leadership in the Church

1 Timothy 3:8–13

Deacons likewise must be men of dignity, not double-tongued, or addicted to much wine or fond of sordid gain but holding to the mystery of the faith with a clear conscience. These men must also first be tested; then let them serve as deacons if they are beyond reproach. Women must likewise be dignified, not malicious gossips, but temperate, faithful in all things. Deacons must be husbands of only one wife, and good managers of their children and their own households. For those who have served well as deacons obtain for themselves a high standing and great confidence in the faith that is in Christ Jesus.

In the Gospels, the elders of Israel are frequently linked with the chief priests and scribes. These were the nation's leaders. This set the precedent for elders in the church. The first use of the word *elder* in reference to the church is in Acts 11:30, *And this they did, sending it in charge of Barnabas and Saul to the elders.* In Acts 14:23, elders were first appointed in every church. In Acts 15:2, elders were associated with the apostles. In Philippians 1:1, Paul refers to the elders as overseers and links them with deacons as the leaders of the church.

In 1 Timothy 3, Paul sets forth the qualifications for elders:

An overseer, then, must be above reproach, the husband of one wife, temperate, prudent, respectable, hospitable, able to teach, not addicted to wine or pugnacious, but gentle, peaceable, free from the love of money. He must be one who manages his own household well, keeping his children under control with all dignity (1 Tim. 3:2–4).

Then in verse 8, Paul begins to list the qualifications for deacons. Elders are required to have the ability to teach, but deacons do not need any specific spiritual gift (1 Tim. 3:2).

It is possible that the first occurrence of the role of a deacon may be in Acts 6 where seven men (not women) were chosen to oversee the administration of caring for Hellenistic widows who were being neglected. This provides strong evidence that God's plan for church leadership resided in the men. If the office of deaconess were to be established, this would have been the perfect time to inaugurate it. The word *serving* in verse one is *diakonia*, and *to serve* in verse two is *diakoneo*. Although it may have been a temporary ministry to those in need, this seems to have set the precedent for the office of deacon. If there were an office of deaconess, why did the Apostles choose men to serve widows.

Although women are praised for their support (Joanna and Susanna in Luke 8:3) and for deeds of kindness and charity (Dorcas in Acts 9:36), it is the men who were to supervise these acts in the church. In Acts 21:8, the Apostle Paul stayed with Philip the evangelist in Caesarea, referring to him as *one of the seven* deacons. The Apostle Paul addresses deacons in Philippians 1:1.

In 1 Timothy 3:8–13, the qualifications for the office of deacon are specified. The word translated *deacon* (*diakonos*) means literally a "humble servant." For the deacons to be eligible for office, they must be: *men of dignity, not double-tongued, not addicted to much wine, not fond of sordid gain, and holding to the mystery of the faith with a clear conscience.*

But then Paul requires them to be tested before they could serve to determine that they are "beyond reproach." If they are found blameless, then they would qualify to serve as deacons. Litfin summarizes that,

> The role of the deacons is to carry out, under the elders' oversight, some of the more menial tasks of the church so that the elders can give their attention to more important things.[134]

Then in verse 12, Paul continues the qualifications, stating, *Deacons must be husbands of one wife and good managers of their children and their own households.* But then it seems unusual for Paul to interrupt the qualifications of deacons to talk about women in verse 11, *Women must likewise be dignified, not malicious gossips, but temperate, faithful in all things.*

The existence of the office of deaconess is strongly debated. Some have questioned whether this is describing the office of deaconess. But he doesn't use the feminine form of deacon. Since the Greek word, *gunē*, can be used for woman or wife, it is more likely that he is referring to the wives of deacons--especially since he continues talking about deacons in the next verse.[135]

A translator's note in the NET Bible states, "The author seems to indicate clearly in the next verse that women are not deacons: "Deacons must be husbands of one wife."[136]

The principle given in 1 Timothy 2:12 appears to be an overarching principle for church life which seems implicitly to limit the role of deacon to men.[137] Baker's Evangelical Dictionary of Biblical Theology states:

> "The women" has been variously interpreted to mean the wives of the deacons, female assistants to the deacons, deaconesses, or women in general. In favor of view 1 is the fact that *gunaikos* [gunaikei'o"][138] occurs also in verses 2 and 12, where it clearly means wife. Second, to return to qualifications for deacons in verses 12-13, and to address the children in verse 12, argues for wives being in view in verse 11."[139]

In Romans 16:1, Paul refers to a woman named Phoebe as a "diakonon of the church" (Rom. 16:1), which can be translated either "servant" or "deacon." But since nothing is said about her role, it cannot be concluded conclusively that she was fulfilling the office of deaconess. She may have just been serving the Lord as part of the church in Rome. But Paul "saw her not as inferior or less capable, but as a trusted and valued member of the Body of Christ."[140] House summarizes:

> If Phoebe ministered to the saints, as is evident from verse 2, then she would be a servant of the church and there is neither need nor warrant to suppose that she occupied or exercised what amounted to

an ecclesiastical office comparable to that of the diaconate.[141]

The role of women in the church is rapidly becoming one of the most controversial issues in western Christianity.[142] Irving Bible Church claims: "Key New Testament passages restricting women's rules were culturally and historically specific, not universal principles for all times and places."[143]

Many denominations today allow women to be pastors, elders, and deacons. There are also instances where women are called deaconesses but do not hold a place on the deacon board. They serve the church, but they do not hold an official position. They are merely given the title.

The office of deacon in the New Testament is an authoritative position, which is closely associated to that of elder. For a woman to hold the office of a deaconess, which would put her in a position of authority over men, would be in violation of Paul's injunction in 1 Timothy 2:12. It appears then that this office is restricted to men. When Paul mentions deacons in 1 Timothy 3:8 and 12, it refers to men. However, wives could assist their deacon-husbands since the office of deacon, unlike that of elder, was not a teaching or governing office in the church and only referred to one aspect of the ministry—service.

12

God's Design or Our Choice

Life is filled with decisions. One of the major roles of parents is to teach their children to make good choices. But throughout our lives we are faced with temptations. It is not a sin to be tempted, but we sin when we give in to the temptation.

> *Let no one say when he is tempted, "I am being tempted by God"; for God cannot be tempted by evil, and He Himself does not tempt anyone. But each one is tempted when he is carried away and enticed by his own lust. Then when lust has conceived, it gives birth to sin; and when sin is accomplished, it brings forth death* (Jam. 1:13–15).

God created each of us as either male or female. Our identity at birth is God's design for us. Homosexuality is immoral and abnormal. It is a denunciation of God's design and is a distortion of the Scriptures. God considers it an abomination to change the gender we were born with, either mentally, overtly, or physically. This is specifically addressed in the following verses:

A woman shall not wear man's clothing, nor shall a man put on a woman's clothing; for whoever does these things is an abomination to the Lord your God (Deut. 22:5).

You shall not lie with a male as one lies with a female; it is an abomination (Lev. 18:22).

God detests homosexuality. Merriam-Webster Dictionary defines *abomination* as "something that causes disgust or hatred."[144] The word *abomination* is used 46 times in the Bible and refers to God's hatred of such things as idolatry, immorality, dishonesty, desecration of the sanctuary, abolishment of sacrifices, pagan sacrifices, and rejection of God's will.

The New Testament also defines homosexuality as sin. Paul states in Romans 1:21 and 22 that the hearts of those who did not honor God or give Him thanks became foolish. Romans 1:25-27 teaches explicitly that homosexuality is a result of a continual rebellion against God.

For they exchanged the truth of God for a lie, and worshiped and served the creature rather than the Creator, who is blessed forever. Amen. For this reason God gave them over to degrading passions; for their women exchanged the natural function for that which is unnatural, and in the same way also the men abandoned the natural function of the woman and burned in their desire toward one another, men with men committing indecent acts and receiving in their own persons the due penalty of their error.

Homosexuality is immoral and unnatural. It interferes with God's creative order. 1 Timothy 1:10 states that it is "contrary to sound teaching." First Corinthians 6:9 states that homosexuals will not inherit the kingdom of God. The sins of unbelievers are defined in many ways. But they are forgiven when they place their faith in Jesus Christ.

Or do you not know that the unrighteous will not inherit the kingdom of God? Do not be deceived; neither fornicators, nor idolaters, nor adulterers, nor effeminate, nor homosexuals, nor thieves, nor the covetous, nor drunkards, nor revilers, nor swindlers, will inherit the kingdom of God. Such were some of you; but you were washed, but you were sanctified, but you were justified in the name of the Lord Jesus Christ and in the Spirit of our God (1 Cor. 6:9–11).

The worship of pagan gods was at times characterized by sex reversal and homosexuality. Unfortunately, this is becoming prevalent in today's society. Thankfully, many are standing against it. Some states are banning gender-changing treatment for minors, such as puberty blockers, hormones, and surgery. Women are opposing competition from transwomen in women's sports.

Homosexuality has become a fad. Many are persuaded to try it. Sexual surgery is sometimes performed without parental consent. A person's genetic inheritance, their biological sex, is an immutable characteristic. It is possible to change a person's outward appearance, including bodily features. But humans cannot change their gender, which was determined at fertilization (genotype) and during embryonic development (phenotype).[145] We cannot undo what God has done! *I will give thanks to You, for I am fearfully and wonderfully made; Wonderful are Your works, And my soul knows it very well* (Psalm 139:14). Homosexuality is both forgivable and able to be rejected as a lifestyle by believers who are filled with the Holy Spirit.

13

It's All about Eve

The biblical role of women begins in the Garden of Eden and continues throughout the Old Testament, the time of Christ, and the present era of the church. It is grounded in the plan of God, beginning with the creation of Adam and Eve. There are two aspects of creation that are essential in understanding the role of women in Scripture—essence and function. Adam and Eve were each created in the image of God (Gen. 1:26), which indicates equality in their essence; yet their distinct functional roles are evident. Adam was created first, which implies certain rights and authority of the firstborn (Gen. 2:7; 1 Tim. 2:13). Eve was created by God from Adam's rib and was given to him as a helpmeet (1 Cor. 11:8-9; Gen. 2:22). Evidence of Adam's headship is apparent in Genesis as he was placed in the garden first (2:8), was given the command not to eat of the tree of knowledge of good and evil (2:17), was promised a helper suitable for him (2:18), and was given the responsibility to initiate the marriage relationship (2:24). This headship continues after the Fall as God calls first to Adam after the eating of the apple (3:9), and later expels him from the garden (3:23).

Because of their sin, the curse resulted in an attempt by them to distort these roles, although the roles of Adam and Eve did not change. Eve would now seek to dominate or control Adam, while Adam would endeavor to lord it over her (Gen. 3:16) (cf. Gen. 4:7). Submission and love (Col. 3:18, 19), which are evidenced by Spirit-filled spouses, are the opposite of what the sin nature is tempted to do in the marriage relationship.

In the Old Testament, women were chosen of God for special ministries (Exo. 15:20; Judg. 4:4, 14; 2 Kings 22:14–20; Est. 2:17). However, it was the men whom God clearly designated as leaders in Israel. Moses chose able men as heads and leaders of the people (Exo. 18:25). The sons of Aaron were consecrated as priests (Exo. 28:41). Men were anointed by God to reign over Israel (1 Sam. 12:13; 15:1).

The New Testament honors women in many significant ways. Jesus' love and respect for women is evident. However, women were not among those chosen to be His disciples. The Scriptures do not teach that Jesus appointed women for church leadership.

Galatians 3:28 teaches that women are equal with men in their position in Christ. The issue in this verse is theological, not experiential. The context of the verse is justification by faith. The death and resurrection of Jesus Christ did not change or eliminate role distinctions or functional differences that were initiated at Creation. Though there are functional distinctions, there is a spiritual equality of men and women in the body of Christ.

The leadership roles in the New Testament church were given to men as evidence of the continuation of God's plan for functional order. Men were to be chosen as pastors, elders, and deacons in the church.

Most who hold to the view that women can teach men today usually fail to consider the last phrase in 1 Timothy 2:11, "but must remain quiet." The argument that women could not teach because the false teachers deceived them is a weak line of reasoning, since the Apostle Paul exhorts women to minister to younger women (Titus 2:3-5). In verse 13, Paul clearly gives the reason for his prohibition—creative order. In 1 Timothy 2:13-15 the arguments of the Apostle parallel the creation, fall, and curse in Genesis 2 and 3. Creative order is to be upheld. Eve was deceived by Satan to reject her divinely ordained role of dependence upon God and her husband in favor of independence. This passage is a warning to women to use self-restraint less they be deceived into forsaking their role.

In addition, when attempting to interpret any verse or passage in the Bible, the finding must be one that agrees with the rest of scriptural teaching on the subject. While men and women who were created in the image of God are equal in essence, and as believers they are equal in their position in Christ, there are clear functional distinctives between them throughout Scripture. The headship of man unmistakably began at creation and continues throughout the Bible. However, this in no way implies the inferiority of women. A husband is to be considerate of his wife's weaker role, while honoring her as a joint heir of the grace of life (1 Pet. 3:7).

There is no evidence in the New Testament of women as pastors in the church assembly. The role distinctions that began at creation continued throughout the Old Testament. They were also evident at the time of Jesus Christ. Even the church age did not change God's design of male headship. The male and female roles are consistent throughout Scripture. A woman's role does not make her inferior. It is designed to protect and bless her.

The Bible attests to the fact that women were created in the image of God, equal in essence with men, and are also considered equal in their position in Christ. However, equality in essence or status before God does not eliminate the biblical hierarchical relationships in the home or in the church. These are mutually exclusive aspects within God's plan. As men in the Old Testament were selected as leaders, priests, and kings in Israel, so men are designated as the leaders of the church and home. God's design and plan for women was initiated in the Garden of Eden and is woven and as having authority in the into the chronicles of history, despite changes in culture or the influence of false teachers. His plan is perfect and is not thwarted by any conflict or opposition.

We gain perspective on this issue by recognizing that the biblical worldview is grounded in the fact that a personal God sovereignly designed an ordered universe to function in a particular way. Crucial to this worldview is the concept of authority. Romans 13:1 tells us that God is the source not simply of all authority but of the very concept of authority.

Within that authority structure, both men and women are given the privilege of serving Him—but in different ways. Simply because Scripture says women can't teach men in a position of authority does not mean that their ministries are unimportant. To Paul, all ministries were significant:

> *"The eye cannot say to the hand, 'I don't need you.' And the head cannot say to the feet, 'I don't need you.' On the contrary, parts of the body that seem to be weaker are indispensable, and the parts that we think are less honorable we treat with special honor"* (1 Cor. 12:21-23a).

From the very beginning, the Bible teaches that men and women are equal in their essence before God but are different in role and function.

Some women seek to justify the fact that they are pastoring a church or teaching men by saying that they have been anointed or called by God. The issue is that God would not call someone to do something that is contrary to His Word. The answer is found in the Word of God, not in someone's experience.

On Larry King Live, Dr. Bob Jones, III, commented:

> And if the Holy Ghost is going to tell us in the Scriptures that a woman is not to usurp authority over a man and is not to pastor a church and be the religious teacher of men, and then he's going to turn around and tell somebody in our generation that it's all right to, then we have God contradicting himself, and that's not any kind of a God who is in control of anything and certainly not the god of the Bible, and so I totally reject the idea that we can have a made-for-today kind of faith.[146]

The headship of man began in the Garden of Eden prior to the fall, was evident in the nation Israel, was recognized by Christ during His earthly ministry, and continues in the church today. God's design and plan for women has not changed with the death and resurrection of Jesus Christ. Men and women are equal in essence, having been created in the image of God, and they are equal in their position in Christ. The function of women in the church and in the home is distinct and unique. It is not secondary or unimportant. It is certainly not inferior.

The role of women is uniquely designed by our loving creator-God. Our femininity, which is given by God, is lost if we attempt to be like a man. God has bestowed upon us the position of greatest influence, richest blessing, and utmost fulfillment, to say nothing of contentment!

Eve continues to impact women today. Her reputation haunts us. Her deception condemns us and keeps us from ministry. But we can restore Eve's distorted image. We can learn from her bad example. Paul didn't forget her, neither should we; but don't misrepresent her either.

14

Finding Our Niche

As women consider what they believe to be the call of God upon their lives, it must be understood that the call should never be in opposition to the role of women as defined in Scripture. The Bible is not to be interpreted through the lens of culture. God does not contradict Himself. The role of women is uniquely designed by our loving Creator-God to place us in a position of greatest influence, richest blessing, and utmost fulfillment.

God has blessed women with a multi-faceted role involving infinite possibilities for serving Him. His plan is perfect. If we feel rejected or stifled, perhaps we are failing to understand that He formulated our role with His infinite wisdom, motivated by His love for us. Or maybe we are taking matters into our own hands instead of trusting Him for our lives. We must be sure there is not bitterness or resentment in our lives. We have so much for which to be thankful. God has designed a role for women that encompasses both protection and blessing. But understanding and accepting that role is essential.

Women are admonished to learn the Word of God. The older women are exhorted to train younger women. Women are to be involved in the teaching and training of children. However, they are not permitted to officially teach men or be in authority over them. In the early church, women had important ministerial roles as older women, widows, and deacon's wives, where they were under the authority of the church leaders as they cared for the needs of women. In fact, every woman who is a believer has a spiritual gift sovereignly given by God. Women are to minister to others using their spiritual gifts in helping to build up the Body of Christ. There are many opportunities for women to serve the Lord.

A great deal of ambiguity results when the doctrine of gender equality in both essence and position in Christ is confused with roles or functions in the church and in the home. Who we are as women is not the issue in this discussion. What we do is. We must not use our own interpretation of Galatians 3:28 or 1 Timothy 2:12 (or a few isolated incidences like Deborah or Priscilla) to formulate a doctrine which gives women authority to teach men or preach in the pulpit. We must be careful that a biblical exception is not used to justify a ministry or attempt to make it the norm in modern-day Christianity. We must look at the verses in their context as well as consider the overall teaching of Scripture on the subject.

Some use the example of a growing church or Bible study attempting to prove that God is blessing a woman who is teaching men. Apparent success in ministry and even the fact that men are growing spiritually are not valid criteria. Nor is giftedness or a well-prepared message proof of God's blessing. God will always bless the Word of God. The Holy Spirit can use the Scriptures in the lives of those who are willing to listen and obey, regardless of the messenger. The issue is not spiritual gifts, ability, or spiritual maturity, but rather the role of women as designed by God.

Some have asked whether women are permitted to teach men in a Bible college or seminary or at a conference. Of course, Paul does not specifically address this in the first century. Some argue that since these are not church settings, it is permitted. It is regrettable that some in the Christian community are basing their view of the role of women on the dictates and examples of a secular society rather than on biblical principles.

But another issue must also be addressed. Since the Scripture teaches that men are designated to be the leaders of the church, it seems apparent that it is the men who must train them. Future leaders of the church need godly men as their examples and as role models for ministry. I studied the book of Esther for many years, wrote a twelve-week Bible study on the book, and taught it numerous times as a course in Bible colleges. But when my husband was preaching through the Bible at the church where he was the pastor, I did not preach on Esther. The issue is not whether women know more on a given topic or could do a better job teaching or preaching. The issue is God's design and plan for women.

Elizabeth Elliot commented on this topic,

> "A Christian woman's true freedom lies on the other side of a very small gate-humble obedience-but that gate leads out into a largeness of life undreamed of by the liberators of the world, to a place where the God-given differentiation between the sexes is not obfuscated but celebrated, where our inequalities are seen as essential to the image of God, for it is in male and female, in male as male and female as female, not as two identical and interchangeable halves, that the image is manifested."[147]

This is not an issue of women breaking the glass ceiling in Christianity. It involves adherence to God's plan for a woman as specified in the Bible--not as inferior, but as protected and specially designed for her role. The impact of history and culture do not change the function of women as defined in the Scriptures.

Don't try to duplicate the role of a man! You are unique! You are special! Enjoy the blessings of being a woman created and designed by God for exceptional purposes. Don't compare yourself to others. Be the best you!

APPENDIX A

Hermeneutics

Christians continue to debate spiritual and functional equality between men and women. Differences abound. The problem is not with the writings of Scripture. Most complementarians and evangelical feminists hold to the Bible's inspiration as well as its authority. The problem is interpretation. Faulty hermeneutics or inconsistent exegesis results in flawed interpretation. Exegesis is the interpretation of the Bible while hermeneutics are the rules by which that interpretation is derived.[148] Therefore, any interpretation of a verse or passage of Scripture is dependent upon the hermeneutics which were used to formulate it.

Defining hermeneutics as "the principles and methods used to interpret Scripture," *Nelson Bible Dictionary* states further that,

> "Bible scholars believe a biblical text must be interpreted according to the language in which it was written, its historical context, the identity and

purpose of the author, its literary nature, and the situation to which it was originally addressed."[149]

The careful and honest use of hermeneutics is essential in the interpretation of the teaching of Scripture regarding the biblical role of women. Without precise interpretation, there can be no correct application. We must not only understand the hermeneutical methods of interpreting Scripture, but we must be faithful and honest in using them accurately and completely. Otherwise, the result will be false doctrine.

The most important rule of Bible interpretation is a determination of the context. Asking the following questions is crucial. What is the subject of the passage? What is the theme of the book? What is the purpose of the book? To whom was it written? An accurate understanding of the context can often prevent errors in interpretation.[150]

In an attempt to document a belief, one can prove almost anything by taking Scripture verses out of context. My favorite illustration as a Bible college instructor was to tell my students that the Bible says, "There is no God." Some would gasp; others had puzzling looks on their faces. Then I asked them to look at Psalm 53:1, which states, "The fool has said in his heart, 'There is no God.'" Knowing the context is essential. Taking verses out of their context can result in either false doctrine or incorrect application, whether by cults or well-meaning Christians.

Even word studies must begin with an evaluation of the context. The meaning of any word is ultimately determined by the context of the verse and passage in which it appears. For example, *salvation* usually refers to eternal life, but not always. In 1 Timothy 2:15, the word *saved*, sometimes translated *preserved*, cannot refer to eternal salvation or else only women who bear children could be saved. That would exclude men, children, barren women, and all other women who are childless. We know from the rest of Scripture that this is not theologically accurate. Therefore, deeper study is needed to determine the meaning of the word from the context.

Staying true to the text is also an important issue in interpretation. Often, the problem is our bias or our own subjectivity. Many times, we approach a passage thinking we already understand it. Without careful study, there is a tendency to read our own meaning into the passage. This is called eisegesis.[151] An example of this is a claim that Priscilla and "Aquila, planted a church 'in their home' (Rom. 16:5), where presumably she taught the Bible, even to other pastors and leaders."[152]

It is true that a church met in the couple's home in Rome. But the passage does not say that they planted the church, nor does it even imply Priscilla ever taught pastors or leaders there. Acts 18:24-26, does say that in Ephesus, Priscilla and Aquila took Apollos aside and "explained to him the way of God more accurately," since he was only acquainted with the baptism of John. This is a far cry from Priscilla teaching pastors and leaders in a church. We must say everything that is in the text—all of it. But we must not go beyond what the Scripture says.

In order to justify our opinion, it is easy to find someone who agrees with our viewpoint. But we must be like the Bereans. These Jews in the synagogue of Berea held the Scriptures in such high regard that they even sought to verify the teachings of the Apostle Paul as he spoke in their synagogue. Acts 17:11 praises these Bereans,

> *Now these were more noble-minded than those in Thessalonica, for they received the word with great eagerness, examining the Scriptures daily to see whether these things were so.*

What wonderful models for believers today! The Word of God is the only source of accuracy. His Word is truth. Every opinion and interpretation must be verified by Scripture or else be rejected. Scripture must be used to define Scripture. The vague passages should be interpreted by considering clear teachings in other parts of the Bible.

There is a danger in formulating a doctrine based on exceptions to a norm in Scripture or using biblical narratives to construct rules for living the Christian life. Simply because an action or practice is recorded in a biblical narrative does not mean the practice is normative or authoritative for believers today. It is only authoritative if Scripture designates it as such.[153] It may be tempting to use Deborah or Priscilla as prototypes, but their narratives cannot be used to formulate a precise model for the biblical role of women in the absence of other Scriptural admonitions.

Differing methods of interpreting Scripture have a decisive impact on one's understanding of the biblical role of women. Some hold to a broad, generalized interpretation of passages regarding the role of women, resulting in an overly strict, legalistic application. An example of this is the broad application of the oft-quoted 1 Corinthians 14:34 phrase, "women are to keep silent in the churches." Some churches use this passage to forbid women to speak in church in any capacity, even refusing to permit them to voice their opinions in church meetings.

On the other end of the spectrum, women are ordained as pastors and elders. For some, gender is not an issue in church leadership. The publishing of egalitarian or gender-neutral Bibles reveals an inclination of some toward gender equality.

Questions about the role of women must be answered from the Scriptures, rather than being derived from tradition or society. Culture changes. Society evolves. But the Word of God endures forever (Matt. 24:35).

Appendix B

Feminists and Complementarians

There are three popular philosophies today concerning the roles of women. It is evident that these positions seem to be grounded in three different points of view regarding Scripture. The first usually denies the inspiration of the Bible, often considering it to be irrelevant. The second view interprets the Bible from a feminist viewpoint in what is an attempt to liberate the Scriptures from its patriarchal bias and oppression of women. The last perspective believes the Bible to be inspired, seeking to interpret it in a precise manner. As a result of their varied views of the Scriptures, the differences between the teachings of these three positions on the role of women are contradictory.

Secular Feminists deny any male headship or authority, often regarding the Genesis account as a myth. They do not accept the Bible as authoritative. They consider men and women to be equal in their roles. Therefore, they believe that these roles are interchangeable in society in the church and in the home.

Christian Feminists (egalitarians) argue that men and women were created equal but lost their equality at the fall. They claim that the headship of man originated as part of the curse. Quoting Galatians 3:28, they believe the work of Christ on the cross restored that equality, overcoming the curse of man's headship. They base the leadership of the church on spiritual gifts and ability, rather than on gender. Specific passages thought to be inconsistent with their view are said to have been misinterpreted.[154] Some claim that evangelical feminists frequently interpret Scripture from a feminist vantage point in what seems to be an attempt to liberate the Bible from its male favoritism and oppression of women. The history and culture of the passages in question become of utmost importance. Their view of Scripture becomes apparent as Russell comments,

> As the contributions to feminist interpretation have continued to grow in volume and maturity – it has become abundantly clear that the scriptures need liberation – not only from existing interpretations but also from the patriarchal bias of the texts themselves.[155]

Conservative Christians (complementarians) believe that God created men and women equal in essence, but with distinct roles. Holding to the headship of Adam before the fall, they believe God intends for men and women to fulfill different gender roles in the church and in the home.

It is clear that differing methods of interpreting Scripture have a decisive impact on one's definition of the role of women in the church and in the family. Various interpretations of biblical passages result in conflicting views about women. Some conservative Christians hold to a broad interpretation of passages regarding the role of women in the church, resulting in an overly strict application of Scripture.

In interpreting the Bible, it is important to determine the meaning of the verse or passage based on its historical, grammatical, and literary contexts. In addition, the interpretation of the biblical text must agree with the teaching of the rest of Scripture on the subject. Care must be taken not to allegorize Scripture, that is search for a hidden or secret code, or a meaning separate from the normal, literal reading. Observation and interpretation must be accurate because without precise interpretation, there can be no correct application.

Tradition often plays a major role in the explanation and application of biblical passages relating to women. Unless the Word of God is considered to be the sole authority in the formulation of a doctrine on the role of women, tradition and society will continue to dictate attitudes and beliefs about women.

The application of the Bible to today's culture must be true to Scripture and be in harmony with the context of the passage. The church must consider how God's unique design and plan for women, as revealed in the Scriptures, affect Christian women today. Specific issues must be addressed from the Bible in response to secular or non-biblical positions. Believers must adequately demonstrate the relevance of the Bible to culture's ever-changing views of a woman's role. Questions must be answered from the Scriptures, rather than relying on tradition or society for the answers. Does God consider women to be inferior to men? Is there any sense in which men and women are portrayed in Scripture as being equal? Are their roles distinctly portrayed in the Bible? Did the Fall of Adam and Eve affect the function of woman as created by God? How do these findings affect the role of women in the church and in the home?

Women today have tremendous influence in the church by virtue of their numbers, their training of their children as future leaders of the church, their effect on their husbands who may be pastors or elders, and their work within the church itself. In many ways, they are the strength and backbone of the church.

There are three primary passages in the New Testament which discuss the behavior of women in the context of church worship: 1 Corinthians 11: 3-16, 1 Corinthians 14:34, and 1 Timothy 2:9- 1. Are these texts to be understood only considering their historical setting or were they intended to be applied to women today?

There appears to be an apparent contradiction in Paul's instructions to women regarding their behavior in the worship assembly. In 1 Corinthians 11, women pray and prophesy. Yet in 1 Corinthians 14 and 1 Timothy 2, they are told to be quiet. The church's application today of these instructions ranges from absolute prohibition of the participation of women in worship services to the ordination of women as pastors. A study of these passages will help us understand the biblical role of women today. In addition, the roles of the older and younger women in Titus 2:3-5 will be discussed. The submission of wives and the meaning of the term *weaker vessel* in 1 Peter 3:1-7 are also important. The issue of deaconesses must be considered in the overall context of church leadership.

A biblical study of the role of women must begin with the creation of Eve as depicted in Genesis 1 and 2. Genesis is the background sketch from which the biblical portrait of a woman is painted.

It is obvious that there is a broad range of beliefs within what has been called Christian feminism. Evangelical egalitarians, however, are on the conservative end of that spectrum. Yet they remain dedicated to equality between men and women in the church and in the home.

Like many evangelical egalitarians, Christian complementarians, some of whom are referred to as hierarchicalists or traditionalists, also hold to a high view of the Scriptures. However, they differ in that they believe God created men and women equal in essence, but with distinct roles. Holding to the headship of Adam before the Fall, they believe God intends for men and women to fulfill different gender roles in the church and in the home. Hoch summarizes the position of Christian complementarians:

> "Hierarchicalists reaffirm the position of traditional Judaism and Christianity that God has determined a functional hierarchy in the home and in the church. There is a role differentiation between male and female. Males are designated as the leaders in the church. Only men are eligible for the office of teaching and ruling elder. In the home, although husbands are to love their wives, wives are to submit themselves to their husbands (Eph. 5:22, 24; Col. 3:18)."[156]

Complementarians are said to show partiality toward men and prejudice against women. Some are even called misogynists for their supposed dislike of women. Others are accused of promoting the abuse of women. Harris calls complementarianism "inconsistent, unjust, and unbiblical."[157] They are also accused of selective literalism. However, Mickelsen believes that it is "tradition, rather than biblical principles that has limited the ministry of women."[158] She claims intelligent women are being driven out of the church as a result.[159]

Scholer explains the error of this approach, noting, "The biblical text one chooses for one's starting point in the study of a doctrine or issue in Scripture becomes the lens through which one looks at all other texts."[160]

Hoch states that evangelical egalitarians believe that "hierarchicalists have misused the texts that seem to support a hierarchy that limits the kinds of ministry women may perform in the church."[161] In July 2010, The Freedom for Christian Women Coalition demanded an apology from the Council on Biblical Manhood and Womanhood for "the misuse of Holy Scripture as it relates to women."[162]

The growing influence of feminism on Christianity is evident today on the Internet and in bookstores. Spiritual and functional equality between men and women continues to be debated. Rogers concludes that the "goal of most evangelical feminists was to prove that traditional interpretations of passages on women's roles were wrong, and that Paul was misunderstood.[163]

Evangelical feminists deny male headship or authority, believing that the fall of man in Genesis 3 led to a sinful hierarchical relationship between man and woman.[164] Quoting Galatians 3:28, they assume the work of Christ on the cross overcame the curse of man's headship, and restored equality between men and women. Jewett calls this verse the "Magna Carta of Humanity."[165] Egalitarians believe husbands and wives should have equal leadership roles in marriage. In addition, Scanzoni and Hardesty claim that Galatians 3:28 teaches that "all social distinctions between men and women should [be] erased in the church."[166] Leadership roles in the church then are said to be determined by spiritual gifts and ability, rather than by gender. However, there continues to be disagreement among complementarians regarding a traditional view of male headship over women in general, and the extent of women's silence in the church.

There are overlaps into philosophies of evangelical egalitarians and complementarians, with extremes tending toward legalism or liberalism. Both derive their philosophies of women from different methods of interpreting Scripture, resulting in conflicting opinions about both the essence and role of women. The same Scripture verses are used to argue both sides of the issue.

The bottom line is biblical interpretation. Christians for Biblical Equality admit that the emphasis of evangelical feminists is usually on the interpretation of Scripture "holistically and thematically."[167] Scholer defines feminist hermeneutics as "a reading of the Biblical text in the light of the oppressive structures of patriarchal society."[168] Their experience and desire for equality becomes the "locus of authority."[169] But Gundry disagrees, claiming that their belief in the full humanity of women is the driving force behind their "advocacy of the rights of women."[170] In his view, the result, not the main cause, is a demand for full equality for women in all levels of society.[171] In either case, they approach Scripture with a preconceived model of womanhood. This then becomes the driving force behind their hermeneutics.

On the other hand, traditional complementarians have been accused of making 1 Timothy 2:11-14 the vantage point from which all of Scripture should be interpreted. Others focus primarily on the silence of women in 1 Corinthians 14:34. Like Galatians 3:28 for the evangelical egalitarians, using one verse as the launching pad for a philosophy of women's ministry distorts it from the onset.

The problem is not with the text of Scripture. Most complementarians and evangelical feminists hold to the Bible's inspiration as well as its authority. Yet each side accuses the other of unreliable interpretation. Discrepancies then are grounded in human opinion resulting from faulty hermeneutics or flawed exegesis.

Appendix C

The Headship of Adam	
Scripture	**Description**
Gen. 1:26	Generic Term "man" used for Adam and Eve
Gen. 2:7	Adam "formed first" (1 Timothy 2:13)
Gen. 2:7	Adam formed "of dust" from the ground
Gen. 2:8, 15	Adam placed in the garden to cultivate it and keep it"
Gen. 2:17	Adam not to eat of "tree of knowledge of good and evil"
Gen. 2:17	Adam warned of spiritual and physical death
Gen. 2:18	"not good for the man [Adam] to be alone"
Gen. 2:18	Adam given "a helper suitable for him"
Gen. 2:21, 22	Adam's rib "fashioned into a woman"
Gen. 2:22	God brought the woman "to the man"
Gen. 2:24	Man to "leave father and mother" "cleave to wife"
Gen. 3:9	The Lord God called to Adam, "Where are you?"
Gen. 3:22	"man has become like one of us, knowing good and evil"
Gen. 3:23	The Lord God *drove the man out* of the garden of Eden

Appendix D

Ruth and Esther

Ruth and Esther are the only two books in the Bible named for women.

The providence of God is an important theme in both books

Both are historical narratives vital to the history of the nation Israel.

Ruth is read by Jews at the Feast of Pentecost; Esther is read at the Feast of Purim

Feasts are important in both books.

Relatives play important roles in each book.

Death is essential to the plot of both stories.

Each story has someone who stood in the way of God's plan.

Ruth was a Gentile woman from a pagan
country who married a Hebrew.

Esther was a young Jewish girl who married
a pagan Gentile king.

Ruth was a widow; Esther was an orphan.

Ruth was an Israeli immigrant; Esther was an exile.

Ruth was a Gentile living among Jews; Esther a Jew
living among Gentiles.

Ruth was a proselyte; Esther influenced proselytes.

Ruth gleaned in a field; Esther ruled in a palace.

Ruth was a poor; Esther was rich.

Ruth was a king's grandmother; Esther was
related to King Saul.

Ruth gave life, Esther ordered death.

Both were living in a land that was not their own.

Both found favor in the eyes of those who saw them.

Both were taken into the homes of relatives.

Both of their relatives were a blessing to others.

Both were women of integrity.

Both were submissive—willing to die in order
to do God's will.

Both were dressed in special garments in order
to make their request.

God redeemed Ruth to perpetuate the line
of our Redeemer, the Lord Jesus Christ.

God saved Esther to protect the nation through whom
the Redeemer would be born.

APPENDIX E

How To Determine God's Will

1. Some general principles.

   a. God's first priority for everyone is to accept Christ as Savior (2 Pet. 3:9).

   b. For believers, God's first objective is that they be controlled, or filled, by the Holy Spirit (Eph. 5:17-18; 1 John 1:9).

   c. The Word of God reveals the will of God. One reason for the 176 verses in Psalm 119 is to teach us to discover God's will from God's Word (Isa. 55:8-9).

   d. Prayer reveals God's will, "If anyone lacks wisdom… ask" (Jam. 1:5).

   e. Faith is essential to pleasing God and discovering His will (Heb. 11:6). The examples given in Hebrews 11 detail a variety of ways people trusted God.

   f. Submission to God is essential, "Not my will but Thine …" (Luke 22:42).

g. The providential leading of God can indicate the will of God (Acts 10). But remember circumstances and even peace can be rationalized.
h. A decision to marry must be the mutual leading of the Lord (Gen. 24:8).
i. The counsel of godly people is important (Pro. 19:20).

2. Questions to test decisions and actions.

   a. Does it glorify God (Matt. 6:1-6; Col. 3:17; 1 Cor. 10:31)?
   b. Does it help believers grow in Christ (1 Cor. 3:1-3; 8:7-13; Rom. 14)?
   c. Does it win a hearing for the gospel (1 Cor. 9:19-23; 5:9-11)?
   d. Does it help me grow spiritually (Phil. 3:5-6, 13; 1 Cor. 9:24-29)?

3. Some reminders.

   a. Maintain a transformed mind regarding your decision (Rom. 12:2), rather than being persuaded by others to conform to the world.
   b. Don't trust your own understanding (Pro. 3:5-6).
   c. Love God. Jesus asked Peter, "Do you love me?" (John 21:15-17). The greatest commandment is to love God (Matt 22:34-40) Love for God is the greatest test in knowing His will. Glorifying God is the greatest motive (Col. 3:17).

Sources

Arndt, W, F. W. Gingrich, F. W. Danker, and W. Bauer, *A Greek-English lexicon of the New Testament and other early Christian literature,* Chicago: University of Chicago Press, 1996.

Barrett, Matthew. *God's Design For Marriage: Celebrating The Beauty Of Gender Roles In 1 Peter 3:1-7,* (The Journal for Biblical Manhood & Womanhood, Spring 2015).

Boa, Kenneth. *All About Eve: Feminism and the Meaning of Equality.* http://bible.org/seriespage/all-about-eve-feminism-and-meaning-equality, 23 August 2010.

Brown, F, S. R. Driver, and C. A. Briggs (2000). *Enhanced Brown-Driver-Briggs Hebrew and English Lexicon* (electronic ed.) (Oak Harbor, WA: Logos Research Systems).

Bromiley, G. W. "Woman" by R. B. Edwards, *International Standard Bible Encyclopedia*

Brunell, Laura, and Elinor Burkett, "**Feminism,**" *Encyclopædia Britannica,* 2010, Encyclopædia Britannica Online.

CBE International, "Men, Women and Biblical Equality"

Carson, D. A. "I Ti 2:9-15," *New Bible Commentary: 21st century edition* (4th ed.), (Leicester, England; Downers Grove, Ill., USA: Inter-Varsity Press, 1994).

Clarke, Adam. Commentary on 1 Corinthians 11:5, *The Adam Clarke Commentary*, https://www.studylight.org/commentaries/acc/1-corinthians-11.html, 1832.

Cornell Law School, *Federal Rules of Evidence*, Rule 801. Definitions, 1992.

Cottrell, Jack. "Christ: A Model for Headship and Submission: A Crucial Verse in 1 Corinthians 11 Overturns Egalitarian Interpretations" *www.cbmw.org/Journal/Vol-2-No-4/Christ-A-Model-for-Headship-and-Submission.*

Cowan, Christopher W. "Rob Bell's 'Feminine Images' for God: A Review of Rob Bell," NOOMA: "She" (Grand Rapids: Zondervan, 2008). *The Council on Biblical Manhood and Womanhood*, www.cbmw.org/Journal/Vol-14-No-1/Rob-Bell-s-Feminine-Images-for-God, 21 August 2010.

Elliott, Elizabeth. "The Essence of Femininity" in *Recovering Biblical Manhood and Womanhood,* John Piper and Wayne Grudem, Eds. (Wheaton, Illinois: Crossway Books, 1991.

Elwell, W. A., and P. W. Comfort, *Tyndale Bible Dictionary*. Tyndale reference library (367). (Wheaton, Ill.: Tyndale House Publishers, 2001).

Feinberg, Charles L. "The Image of God" in *Bibliotheca Sacra* 129/515 (July 72).

Geisler, Norman, and Ron Rhodes, *Conviction Without Compromise*, Eugene, ORE: Harvest House Publishers, 2008.

Greidanus, Sidney. "Preaching Christ from the Narrative of the Fall," *Bibliotheca Sacra Volume 161* (Dallas Theological Seminary, 2004; 2005), vnp.161.643.266. *BSac* 161:643 (July 2004).

Gundry, Stanley N. "Response to Pinnock, Nicole and Johnston, *Women, Authority and the Bible*," ed. Alvera Michelsen (Downers Grove, Ill: InterVarsity Press, 1986).

Harris, R. Laird, Gleason Leonard Archer, and Bruce K. Waltke, *Theological Wordbook of the Old Testament*, electronic ed. (Chicago: Moody Press, 1999, c1980).

Jamieson, Robert, A. R. Faussett and David Brown, *A Commentary Critical and Explanatory on the Whole Bible, Vol. II, "1 Tim. 2:14"* (Oak Harbor, WA: Logos Research Systems, 1997).

James, Carolyn Custis. "The Return of the Ezer," www.carolyncustisjames.com/2005/12/06/the-return-of-the-ezer/ (March 98,2019).

Jewett, Paul K. *Man as Male and Female* (Grand Rapids: Wm. B. Eerdmans Publishing Co., 1975).

Josephus, F., and W. Whiston, *The works of Josephus: Complete and unabridged, Book 2:25 (199)* (Peabody: Hendrickson, 1996), electronic edition.

Geneva Study Bible. http://bible.cc/1_timothy/2-14.htm. 2/12/2011.

Gower, R., & Wright, F. *The New Manners and Customs of Bible Times* (Chicago: Moody Press, 1997).

Grudem, Wayne. "Does *Kephal* ('Head') Mean 'Source' Or 'Authority Over' in Greek Literature? A Survey of 2,336 Examples," *Trinity Journal* ns 6.1 (Spring 1985).

Harris, Alisa. Hillsdale College "What is Biblical Egalitarianism? " Freeing our Fellow Workers in Christ: Christianity's Message of Gender Equality: "Complementarianism is inconsistent, unjust and unbiblical" April 4, 2007, page 10 Reporter at World Magazine

Hoch, Carl B., Jr., "The Role of Women in the Church: A Survey of Current Approaches," *Grace Theological Journal* 08:2 (Fall 1987).

Hodge, Charles. *Systematic Theology* (Vol. 3), (Oak Harbor, WA: Logos Research Systems).

Holladay, W. L. *A concise Hebrew and Aramaic Lexicon of the Old Testament* (Leiden: Brill 1971).

House, H. Wayne. "Should a Woman Prophesy or Preach before Men?" *Bibliotheca Sacra*, April-June 1988.

_____. "A Biblical View of Women in the Ministry, Part 3: The Speaking of Women and the Prohibition of the Law" in *Bibliotheca Sacra*, Vol. 145, #579.

Kassian, Mary A. *Women, Creation, and the Fall* (Westchester, Il: Crossway Books, 1990).

Keathley, J. Hampton, III, "Prophecies of the Birth of Christ," bible.org/article/prophecies-birth-christ.

Keil, C. F., and F. Delitzsch, "Gen. 3:15," *Commentary on the Old Testament.* (1:55-67). (Peabody, MA: Hendrickson, 2002).

CNN transcript, Larry King Live: *Should Women Be Pastors?* - June 14, 2000.

Knight, George W., III. "The New Testament Teaching on the Role Relationship of Male and Female with Special Reference to the Teaching/Ruling Functions in the Church" www.etsjets. org/files/JETS-PDFs/18/18-2/18-2-pp081-091_JETS.pdf.

_____. *The Pastoral Epistles: A Commentary on the Greek Text* (Grand Rapids, Mich.; Carlisle, England: W.B. Eerdmans; Paternoster Press, 1992).

Kroeger, Catherine Clark, "Sexual Identity in Corinth: Paul Faces a Crisis. https://studylib.net/doc/8130060/understanding-1-corinthians-11-2-16-in-light-of-culture-and.

Lagass, P. "Geminism," *The Columbia encyclopedia* (6th ed.), (New York; Detroit: Columbia University Press; Sold and distributed by Gale Group, 2000), electronic version.

Lange, J. P., P. Schaff, T. Lewis and A. Gosman, *A Commentary on the Holy Scriptures: Genesis*. (Bellingham, WA: Logos Research Systems, Inc., 2008).

Liddell, H. G. *A Lexicon : Abridged from Liddell and Scott's Greek-English Lexicon* (Oak Harbor, WA: Logos Research Systems, Inc., 1996).

Litfin, A. Duane. "1 Timothy," *The Bible Knowledge Commentary: An Exposition of the Scriptures* (Wheaton, IL: Victor Books, 1983).

Lowery, D. K. "1 Corinthians" in *The Bible Knowledge Commentary: An Exposition of the Scriptures,* J. F. Walvoord & R. B. Zuck (Eds.), (Vol. 2, p. 541), Wheaton, IL: Victor Books, 1985.

Louw, J. P., and E. A. Nida, Greek-English Lexicon of the New Testament: Based on semantic domains, New York: United Bible societies, 1996.

MacArthur, John. "Head Coverings for Women," *Grace to You* https://www.gty.org/library/bibleqnas-library/QA0219/head-coverings-for-women, July 8, 2020.

Mays, J. L. "I Ti. 2:8," *Harper's Bible Commentary* (San Francisco: Harper & Row, 1996).

Merriam-Webster Dictionary: www.merriam-webster.com/dictionary

McComiskey, Thomas E. "137 אֱנוֹשׁ," *Theological Wordbook of the Old Testament*, R. L. Harris, G. L. Archer and B. K. Waltke (Chicago: Moody Press, 1999), electronic version.

Melick, Richard R., Jr. "Women Pastors: What Does the Bible Teach?"

Merrill, E. H. "The Book of Ruth: Narration and Shared Themes," *Bibliotheca Sacra*, 142:566, April 1985.

McQuilkin, J. Robertson. "Limits of Cultural Interpretation," *Journal of Evangelical Theology* (JETS 23/2 (June 1980).

Michael, James A., and F. Stitzinger, "Genesis 1-3 and the Male/Female Role Relationship" in *Grace Theological Journal* 2/1 (Spring 1982).

Mickelsen, Alvera. "An Egalitarian Response," Women in Ministry: Four Views, Bonnidell Clouse and Robert G. Clouse, eds., Downers Grove, Ill: InterVarsity Press, 1989.

Radmacher, E.D., R. B. Allen and H. W. House, *Nelson's New Illustrated Bible Commentary* (Nashville: T. Nelson Publishers, 1999).

Richards, L. O. *The Bible Readers Companion* (Wheaton: Victor Books, 1991, Electronic edition).

Rogers, Mark. "Whence Evangelical Feminism" A Review of Pamela D. H. Cochran, *Evangelical Feminism, the Council on Biblical Manhood and Womanhood,* www.cbmw.org/Journal/Vol-14-No-2/Whence-Evangelical-Feminism (March 3, 2011).

Russell, Letty M., ed., *Feminist Interpretation of the Bible*, (Louisville: Westminster Press, 1985).

Sailhamer, John. "Genesis," in *Expositor's Bible Commentary*, vol. 2, ed. Frank E. Gæbelein (Grand Rapids: Zondervan, 1990).

Scanzoni, Letha, and Nancy Hardesty, *All We're Meant to Be* (Waco, TX: Word Books, 1974).

Scholer, David M. "Feminist Hermeneutics And Evangelical Biblical Interpretation" JETS 30/4 (December 1987), 408, *Journal of the Evangelical Theological Society*, (Lynchburg, VA: JETS, 1998, electronic edition by Galaxie Software.

_____. "1 Timothy 2:9-15 and the Place of Women in the Church's Ministry," *Women, Authority and the Bible*, ed. Alvera Michelsen (Downers Grove, Ill: InterVarsity Press, 1986).

Schultz, Samuel J. "The Unity of the Race," *Bibliotheca Sacra*, electronic edition. (Dallas, TX: Dallas Theological Seminary, 1998). Bib Sac V113:449 Jan 56.

Silbar, Jeff, and Larry Henley, "Wind Beneath My Wings" was written in 1982 by the songwriting duo of. Wind Beneath My Wings lyrics © BMG Rights Management, Warner Chappell Music.

Smith, Jerome H. *The New Treasury of Scripture Knowledge,* Nashville TN: Thomas Nelson, 1992; (Published in electronic form, 1996).

Spence-Jones, H. D. M., ed. (1909), *The Pulpit Commentary:* "Genesis," (Bellingham, WA: Logos Research Systems, Inc., 2004).

Strauch, Alexander. *Men and Women, Equal Yet Different* (Littleton, CO: Lewis and Roth Publishers, 1999).

Strong, J. A Concise Dictionary of the Words in the Greek Testament and The Hebrew Bible, Vol. II (Bellingham, WA: Logos Research Systems, 2009.

Sumner, Sarah. *Men and Women in the Church* ((Downers Grove: Inter-Varsity Press, 2003).

Swanson, James A. "Adam," Dictionary of Biblical Languages with Semantic Domains: Hebrew (OT), (Faithlife, 1997).

Swindoll, Charles R. *Wisdom for the Way.* (Thomas Nelson, Inc., 2010). *The NET Bible First Edition* (Biblical Studies Press, 2006).

Study Light Bible Commentaries, "1 Peter 3:7," *Commentary by A. R. Faussett.* studylight.org/commentaries/eng/jfb/1-peter.htm.

Unger, M. F., R. K. Harrison, Howard F. Vos, and Cyril J. Barber, "Jehovah" in *The New Unger's Bible dictionary* (Rev. and updated ed.), (Chicago: Moody Press, 2006).

Vine, W. E., M. F. Unger & W. White, Jr., *Vine's Complete Expository Dictionary of Old and New Testament Words,* Vol. 2, Nashville, TN: T. Nelson, 1996.

Waltke, Bruce K. "1 Corinthians 11:2-16: An Interpretation," *Bibliotheca Sacra,* Vol 135 537, January-March 1978.

Walvoord, J. F., and R. B. Zuck, ed., "Re 22:19-19," *The Bible Knowledge Commentary: An Exposition of the Scriptures* (Wheaton, IL: Victor Books, 1983).

Wilson, Kenneth T. "Should Women Wear Headcoverings?" Roy B. Zuck, ed. *Vital Biblical Issues: Examining Problem Passages of the Bible.*

Youngblood, R. F., F. F. Bruce, and R. K. Harrison, "1 Peter 3:7," *Nelson's New Illustrated Bible Dictionary,* (Nashville, TN: Thomas Nelson, Inc., 1995).

Zuck, Roy B. *Basic Bible Interpretation* (Colorado Springs: David C. Cook, 1991), 20.

Zuck, Roy, ed. Vital Biblical Issues: Examining Problem Passages of the Bible, Wipf and Stock Publishers, 1994.

Endnotes

1   F. Josephus and W. Whiston, *The works of Josephus: Complete and unabridged, Book 2:25 (199)* (Peabody: Hendrickson, 1996), electronic edition.

2   Laura Brunell and Elinor Burkett, "**Feminism,**" *Encyclopædia Britannica*, 2010, Encyclopædia Britannica Online: https://www.britannica.com/topic/feminism.

3   P. Lagass, "Geminism," *The Columbia encyclopedia* (6th ed.), (New York; Detroit: Columbia University Press; Sold and distributed by Gale Group, 2000), electronic version.

4   Ibid.

5   Appendix A: Hermeneutics explains how to interpret the Bible.

6   James A. Swanson, "Adam," Dictionary of Biblical Languages with Semantic Domains.

7   Kenneth Boa. *All About Eve: Feminism and the Meaning of Equality.* http://bible.org/seriespage/all-about-eve-feminism-and-meaning-equality, 23 August 2010.

8   Michael F. Stitzinger, "Genesis 1-3 and the Male/Female Role Relationship" in *Grace Theological Journal* 2/1 (Spring 1982), 24.

9   Charles L. Feinberg, "The Image of God" in *Bibliotheca Sacra* 129/515 (July 72), 237.

[10] R. Laird Harris, Gleason Leonard Archer, and Bruce K. Waltke, *Theological Wordbook of the Old Testament*, electronic ed. (Chicago: Moody Press, 1999, c1980), 127.

[11] Ibid.

[12] Christopher W. Cowan, "Rob Bell's 'Feminine Images' for God: A Review of Rob Bell," NOOMA: "She" (Grand Rapids: Zondervan, 2008). *The Council on Biblical Manhood and Womanhood*, www.cbmw.org/Journal/Vol-14-No-1/Rob-Bell-s-Feminine-Images-for-God, 21 August 2010.

[13] John Sailhamer, "Genesis," in *Expositor's Bible Commentary*, vol. 2, ed. Frank E. Gæbelein (Grand Rapids: Zondervan, 1990), 38.

[14] M. F. Unger, R. K. Harrison, Howard F. Vos, and Cyril J. Barber, "Jehovah" in *The New Unger's Bible dictionary* (Rev. and updated ed.), (Chicago: Moody Press, 2006).

[15] This issue will be addressed in more detail later in the study of both 1 Corinthians 11 and Ephesians 5.

[16] Samuel J. Schultz, "The Unity of the Race," *Bibliotheca Sacra*, electronic edition. (Dallas, TX: Dallas Theological Seminary, 1998). Bib Sac V113:449 Jan 56, p. 48.

[17] H. D. M. Spence-Jones, ed. (1909), *The Pulpit Commentary:* "Genesis," (Bellingham, WA: Logos Research Systems, Inc., 2004), 46.

[18] W. A. Elwell and P. W. Comfort, *Tyndale Bible Dictionary*. Tyndale reference library (367). (Wheaton, Ill.: Tyndale House Publishers, 2001).

[19] Ibid.

[20] Spence-Jones, "Genesis," 51.

[21] Boa, "All About Eve."

22 Carolyn Custis James, "The Return of the Ezer," www.carolyncustisjames.com/2005/12/06/the-return-of-the-ezer/ (March 98,2019).

23 Ibid.

24 F. Brown, S. R. Driver, and C. A. Briggs (2000). *Enhanced Brown-Driver-Briggs Hebrew and English Lexicon* (electronic ed.) (Oak Harbor, WA: Logos Research Systems), 124.

25 Sidney Greidanus, "Preaching Christ from the Narrative of the Fall," *Bibliotheca Sacra Volume 161* (Dallas Theological Seminary, 2004; 2005), vnp.161.643.266. *BSac* 161:643 (July 2004), 266.

26 Thomas E. McComiskey, "137 אֱנוֹשׁ *Theological Wordbook of the Old Testament*, R. L. Harris, G. L. Archer and B. K. Waltke (Chicago: Moody Press, 1999), electronic version.

27 J. Strong, A Concise Dictionary of the Words in the Greek Testament and The Hebrew Bible, Vol. II (Bellingham, WA: Logos Research Systems, 2009), 78.

28 Ibid.

29 Alexander Strauch, *Men and Women, Equal Yet Different* (Littleton, CO: Lewis and Roth Publishers, 1999), 25.

30 Robert Jamieson, A. R. Faussett and David Brown, *A Commentary Critical and Explanatory on the Whole Bible, Vol. II, "1 Tim. 2:14"* (Oak Harbor, WA: Logos Research Systems, 1997), 408.

31 Boa, "All about Eve."

32 Cornell Law School, *Federal Rules of Evidence*, Rule 801. Definitions, 1992, www.law.cornell.edu/uscode/html/uscode28a/usc

_sec_28a _04000801----000-.html. Rule 801. Definitions, 1992.

33 A. Duane Litfin, "1 Timothy," *The Bible Knowledge Commentary: An Exposition of the Scriptures* (1 Ti 2:14) (Wheaton, IL: Victor Books, 1983).

34 *Geneva Study Bible.* http://bible.cc/1_timothy/2-14.htm. 2/12/2011.

35 StudyLight Bible Commentaries, "1 Timothy 2," *Wesley's Explanatory Notes.* studylight.org/commentaries/eng/wen/1-timothy-2.html

36 StudyLight Bible Commentaries, "1 Peter 3:7," *Commentary by A. R. Faussett.* studylight.org/commentaries/eng/jfb/1-peter.htm.

37 J. L. Mays, "I Ti. 2:8," *Harper's Bible Commentary* (San Francisco: Harper & Row, 1996).

38 D. A. Carson, "I Ti 2:9-15," *New Bible Commentary: 21st century edition* (4th ed.), (Leicester, England; Downers Grove, Ill., USA: Inter-Varsity Press, 1994).

39 Jamieson, Fausset and Brown, A Commentary Critical and Explanatory on the Bible, 408.

40 L. O. Richards, *The Bible Readers Companion* (Wheaton: Victor Books, 1991, Electronic edition) 834.

41 J. F. Walvoord and R. B. Zuck, ed., "Re 22:19-19," *The Bible Knowledge Commentary: An Exposition of the Scriptures* (Wheaton, IL: Victor Books, 1983).

42 R. L. Harris, G. L. Archer, and B. K. Waltke, *Theological Wordbook of the Old Testament* (electronic ed.) (10). (Chicago: Moody Press, 1999). *anthropos*

43 R. L. Harris, G. L. Archer, and B. K. Waltke, "Adam," *Theological Wordbook of the Old Testament* (electronic ed.) (10). (Chicago: Moody Press, 1999).

44 Boa, All About Eve.

45   Ibid.

46   E. D. Radmacher, R. B. Allen and H. W. House, *Nelson's New Illustrated Bible Commentary* "Gen 3:15," (Nashville: T. Nelson Publishers, 1999).

47   J. P. Lange, P. Schaff, T. Lewis and A. Gosman, *A Commentary on the Holy Scriptures: Genesis.* (Bellingham, WA: Logos Research Systems, Inc., 2008), 235.

48   J. Hampton Keathley III, "Prophecies of the Birth of Christ," bible.org/article/prophecies-birth-christ

49   "Genesis 3:16," *The NET Bible First Edition* (Biblical Studies Press, 2006).

50   W. L. Holladay, A concise Hebrew and Aramaic Lexicon of the Old Testament (Leiden: Brill 1971), 280.

51   https://sermons.logos.com/sermons/11050-he-shall-rule-over-you

52   C. F. Keil and F. Delitzsch, "Gen. 3:15," *Commentary on the Old Testament.* (1:55-67). (Peabody, MA: Hendrickson, 2002).

53   "Genesis 3:14," *The NET Bible.*

54   Ibid, 3:16.

55   Mary A. Kassian, *Women, Creation, and the Fall* (Westchester, Il: Crossway Books, 1990), 27.

56   CBE International, "Men, Women and Biblical Equality" www.cbeinternational.org/resource/men-women-and-biblical-equality/.

57   Boa, "All About Eve."

58   Jamieson, Fausset and Brown, *A Commentary Critical and Explanatory on the Whole Bible* (1 Ti 2:14) (Oak Harbor, WA: Logos Research Systems, Inc., 1997).

59 The word order in the Hebrew is, "Then Miriam spoke, and Aaron, against Moses…"

60 E. H. Merrill, "The Book of Ruth: Narration and Shared Themes," *Bibliotheca Sacra*, 142:566, April 1985, 135.

61 Ibid.

62 Walvoord and Zuck, eds. *The Bible Knowledge Commentary: An Exposition of the Scriptures* (Is 3:10–12), (Wheaton, IL: Victor Books, 1983).

63 See Appendix D for a Comparison of the Book of Ruth and the Book of Esther.

64 G. W. Bromiley, "Woman" by R. B. Edwards, *International Standard Bible Encyclopedia* 4:1094.

65 Boa, "All About Eve."

66 Richard R. Melick, Jr., "Women Pastors: What Does the Bible Teach?" http://www.sbc.net/aboutus/faqs.asp#2

67 Ibid.

68 In the Greek language, the word *woman* can refer to either a single or married woman. The context determines whether the word should be translated *woman* or *wife*.

69 Jack Cottrell. "Christ: A Model for Headship and Submission: A Crucial Verse in 1 Corinthians 11 Overturns Egalitarian Interpretations" *www.cbmw.org/Journal/Vol-2-No-4/Christ-A-Model-for-Headship-and-Submission*. Retrieved 8/3/08. Footnote in Cottrell: This point is explained very well by Karl Barth in Church Dogmatics III/4, trans. A. T. Mackay et al. Edinburgh: T. & T. Clark, 1961, 173.

70 George W. Knight, III, "The New Testament Teaching on the Role Relationship of Male and Female with Special Reference to the Teaching/Ruling Functions in the Church" www.etsjets.org/files/ JETS-PDFs/18/18-2/18-2-pp081-091_JETS.pdf, 86.

71 House, H. Wayne. "Should a Woman Prophesy or Preach before Men?" *Bibliotheca Sacra*, April-June 1988.

72 Wayne Grudem, "Does *Kephal* ('Head') Mean 'Source' Or 'Authority Over' in Greek Literature? A Survey of 2,336 Examples," *Trinity Journal* ns 6.1 (Spring 1985), 53.

73 Grudem, *Kephal*, 53.

74 D.K. Lowery "1 Corinthians," J. F. Walvoord & R. B. Zuck, eds., *The Bible Knowledge Commentary: An Exposition of the Scriptures* (Vol. 2). (Wheaton, IL: Victor Books, 1985), 259.

75 Ibid.

76 John MacArthur, "Head Coverings for Women," *Grace to You* https://www.gty.org/library/bibleqnas-library/QA0219/head-coverings-for-women, July 8, 2020.

77 Ibid.

78 Kroeger, Catherine Clark, "Sexual Identity in Corinth: Paul Faces a Crisis. https://studylib.net/doc/8130060/understanding-1-corinthians-11-2-16-in-light-of-culture-and. Accessed July 18, 2020.

79 Gower, R., & Wright, F. *The New Manners and Customs of Bible Times* (Chicago: Moody Press, 1997).

80 Lowery, "1 Corinthians."

81 Bruce K. Waltke, "1 Corinthians 11:2-16: An Interpretation," *Bibliotheca Sacra,* , Vol 135 537, January-March 1978, p. 49.

82 Adam Clarke, Commentary on 1 Corinthians 11:5, The Adam Clarke Commentary, https://www.studylight.org/commentaries/acc/1-corinthians-11.html, 1832.

83 "What Does the Bible Say About Proper Dress?" *Christian Bible Reference Site*, www.christianbiblereference.org/faq_dress.htm 6/25/2022

84   Roy Zuck, ed. Vital Biblical Issues: Examining Problem Passages of the Bible, Wipf and Stock Publishers, 1994.

85   *The NET Bible, First Edition;* Biblical Studies Press, 2005.

86   Bruce K. Waltke, "1 Cor 11," 55.

87   D. K. Lowery, "1 Corinthians," 530.

88   Melick, "Women Pastors: What Does the Bible Teach?"

89   Kenneth T. Wilson, "Should Women Wear Headcoverings?" Roy Bo. Zuck, ed. *Vital Biblical Issues: Examining Problem Passages of the Bible,* 171.

90   Kenneth T. Wilson, "Should Women Wear Headcoverings?" Roy B. Zuck, ed. *Vital Biblical Issues: Examining Problem Passages of the Bible,* 171.

91   Louw and Nida, Greek-English Lexicon of the New Testament.

92   W. Arndt, F. W. Gingrich, F. W. Danker, and W. Bauer, *A Greek-English lexicon of the New Testament and other early Christian literature,* Chicago: University of Chicago Press, 1996.

93   Arndt, Gingrich, Danker, & Bauer.

94   D. K. Lowery, "1 Corinthians," *The Bible Knowledge Commentary.*

95   Biblical Studies Press, The NET Bible First Edition, 2005.

96   *Wayne Grudem, Prophecy and Teaching, Journal of Evangelical Theological Society, JETS 30:1, March 1987, p. 12.*

97   Knight, 88, accessed 7/25/2018.

98   Jerome H. Smith, *The New Treasury of Scripture Knowledge,* Nashville TN: Thomas Nelson, 1992; (Published in electronic form, 1996), 1344.

99   D. A. Carson, *New Bible Commentary: 21st Century Edition,* 4th. Ed., Downers Grove, Ill: Inter-Varsity Press, 1994.

100 Norman Geisler and Ron Rhodes, *Conviction Without Compromise*, Eugene, ORE: Harvest House Publishers, 2008, p. 342.

101 Geisler and Rhodes, *Conviction Without Compromise*, p. 342.

102 Lowery, D. K. (1985). 1 Corinthians. The Bible Knowledge Commentary, 541.

103 Radmacher, Allen and House, "1 Cor. 14:34, "*Nelson's New Illustrated Bible Commentary*,

104 Grudem, Prophecy and Teaching, JETS, p. 12

105 Biblical Studies Press. (2005). The NET Bible First Edition; Bible. English. NET Bible.

106 W. E. Vine, M. F. Unger & W. White, Jr., *Vine's Complete Expository Dictionary of Old and New Testament Words,* Vol. 2, Nashville, TN: T. Nelson, 1996, p 606.

107 http://freecwc.blogspot.com, accessed July 22, 2020.

108 http://hungryheart100.tripod.com/sitebuildercontent /sitebuilderfiles/fcwcassociatebaptispresschristiansdemant dapologyforantiwomenteaching.pdf.pdf.

109 Melick, "Women Pastors: What Does the Bible Teach?"

110 Gromacki,11.

111 Charles Hodge, *Systematic Theology* (Vol. 3), (Oak Harbor, WA: Logos Research Systems, Inc.), 377.

112 Jeff Silbar and Larry Henley, "Wind Beneath My Wings" was written in 1982 by the songwriting duo of. Wind Beneath My Wings lyrics © BMG Rights Management, Warner Chappell Music, Inc.

113 Hodge, Systematic Theology, 377.

114 Artemis, considered to be the equivalent of the Roman goddess Diana, was said to be the daughter of Zeus and Leto,

and the twin sister of Apollo. The Greek goddess Minerva was later equated with Artemis.

[115] Litfin, The Bible Knowledge Commentary, 1 Tim. 4:11.

[116] "What does the Bible say about women pastors?" www.gotquestions.org/women-pastors.html 7/18/2022

[117] George W. Knight, *The Pastoral Epistles: A Commentary on the Greek Text* (Grand Rapids, Mich.; Carlisle, England: W.B. Eerdmans; Paternoster Press, 1992), 140.

[118] H. Wayne House, "A Biblical View of Women in the Ministry, Part 3: The Speaking of Women and the Prohibition of the Law" in *Bibliotheca Sacra*, Vol. 145, #579, 314.

[119] House, 317.

[120] H. G. Liddell, *A Lexicon : Abridged from Liddell and Scott's Greek-English Lexicon* (Oak Harbor, WA: Logos Research Systems, Inc., 1996), 296.

[121] www.gotquestions.org/women-pastors.html

[122] bible.org/seriespage/15-all-about-eve-feminism-and-meaning-equality

[123] Knight, The Pastoral Epistles, 84-5.

[124] Mcquilkin, "Limits of Cultural Interpretation," 115.

[125] J. P. Louw and E. A. Nida (1996), *Greek-English lexicon of the New Testament: based on semantic domains* (electronic ed. of the 2nd edition., Vol. 1, 108). (New York: United Bible Societies).

[126] J. Strong, (2009). In A Concise Dictionary of the Words in the Greek Testament and The Hebrew Bible.

[127] Louw and Nida, "train," Greek-English Lexicon of the New Testament.

[128] Charles R. Swindoll, *Wisdom for the Way.* (Thomas Nelson, Inc., 2010) 269.

[129] The Hebrew word מוּסָר (*musar*) means discipline, or correction. Discipline is achieved by means of observation, instruction, verbal admonition, and or physical chastisement. The goal of discipline is moral education which produces self-control, submissiveness and wisdom. *Musar* occurs in Proverbs 1:2, 3, 7, 8; 3:11; 4:1, 13; 5:12, 23; 6:23; 7:22; 8:33; 10:17; 12:1; 13:1, 18, 24; 15:5, 10, 32, 33; 16:22; 19:20, 27; 22:15; 23:12, 13, 23; 24:32.

[130] Swindoll, Wisdom for the Way, 248.

[131] Matthew Barrett, *God's Design For Marriage: Celebrating The Beauty Of Gender Roles In 1 Peter 3:1-7,* (The Journal for Biblical Manhood & Womanhood, Spring 2015), 61.

[132] Radmacher, Allen, and House, "1 Peter 3:7," *Nelson's New illustrated Bible Commentary.*

[133] R. F. Youngblood, F. F. Bruce, and R. K. Harrison, "1 Peter 3:7," *Nelson's New Illustrated Bible Dictionary*, (Nashville, TN: Thomas Nelson, Inc., 1995).

[134] *The Bible Knowledge Commentary: An Exposition of the Scriptures,* eds. John F. Walvoord & Roy B. Zuck (Vol. 2). (Wheaton, IL: Victor Books, 1985), a. d. "1 Timothy," 737.

[135] The NET Bible First Edition, "1 Timothy," (Biblical Studies Press, 2005).

[136] Ibid.

[137] Ibid.

[138] http://www.biblestudytools.com/lexicons/greek/nas/gunaikeios.html

[139] http://www.biblestudytools.com/dictionaries/bakers-evangelical-dictionary/deacon-deaconess.html 7/18/2022

[140] https://www.gotquestions.org/women-deacons.html 7/18/2022

[141] House, *Bibliotheca Sacra,* Part 4, 389.

[142] https://www.scribd.com/document/61493206/The-Role-of -Women-in-the-Church

[143] https://s3.amazonaws.com/ibcmedia/media/docs/women_ ministry_IBC.pdf

[144] https://www.merriam-webster.com/dictionary/abomination

[145] https://can-sg.org/frequently-asked-questions/can-humans-change-sex/#:~:text=No.,%2C%20diet%2C%20friends%20 or%20careers. Accessed 9/10/2023.

[146] CNN transcript, Larry King Live: *Should Women Be Pastors?* - June 14, 2000.

[147] Elizabeth Elliott, "The Essence of Femininity" in *Recovering Biblical Manhood and Womanhood,* John Piper and Wayne Grudem, Eds. (Wheaton, Illinois: Crossway Books, 1991), 398-99.

[148] Roy B. Zuck, *Basic Bible Interpretation* (Colorado Springs: David C. Cook, 1991), 20.

[149] R. F., Youngblood, F. F. Bruce and R. K. Harrison, eds. "Hermeneutics," *Nelson's New Illustrated Bible Dictionary* (Nashville: Thomas Nelson Publishers, 1995), electronic version.

[150] Youngblood, Bruce and Harrison, "Interpretation of the Bible."

[151] Youngblood, Bruce and Harrison, "Eisegesis."

[152] Sarah Sumner, *Men and Women in the Church* ((Downers Grove: Inter-Varsity Press, 2003), 52.

153   J. Robertson McQuilkin, "Limits of Cultural Interpretation," *Journal of Evangelical Theology* (JETS 23/2 (June 1980) 113-124).

154   Kenneth Boa, "All About Eve: Feminism and the Meaning of Equality," Bible.org, accessed September 28, 2010. http://bible.org/seriespage/all-about-eve-feminism-and-meaning-equality,

155   Letty M. Russell, ed., *Feminist Interpretation of the Bible*, (Louisville: Westminister Press, 1985),11.

156   Carl B. Hoch, Jr., "The Role of Women in the Church: A Survey of Current Approaches," *Grace Theological Journal* 08:2 (Fall 1987) 241-251, 246.

157   Alisa Harris – Hillsdale College "What is Biblical Egalitarianism? " Freeing our Fellow Workers in Christ: Christianity's Message of Gender Equality: "Complementarianism is inconsistent, unjust and unbiblical" April 4, 2007 page 10 Reporter at World Magazine

158   Alvera Mickelsen, "An Egalitarian Response," Women in Ministry: Four Views, Bonnidell Clouse and Robert G. Clouse, eds., Downers Grove, Ill: InterVarsity Press, 1989, p. 61.

159   Ibid, 63

160   David Scholer, "1 Timothy 2:9-15 and the Place of Women in the Church's Ministry," *Women, Authority and the Bible*, ed. Alvera Michelsen (Downers Grove, Ill: InterVarsity Press, 1986), 193-219.

161   Carl B. Hoch, Jr., "The Role of Women in the Church: A Survey of Current Approaches, *Grace Theological Journal* 08:2 (Fall 1987) 241-251,242.

162   "Demand for Apology from the Council on Biblical Manhood and Biblical Womanhood," *Baptist Women for Equality Blog*, posted on July 25, 2010, accessed 3/5/2011. http://

bwebaptistwomenforequality.wordpress.com/2010/07/25/
demand-for-apology-from-the-council-on-biblical-
manhood-and-biblical-womanhood/

[163]   Mark Rogers, "Whence Evangelical Feminism" A Review of
Pamela D. H. Cochran, *Evangelical Feminism, the Council on
Biblical Manhood and Womanhood,* www.cbmw.org/Journal/
Vol-14-No-2/Whence-Evangelical-Feminism <u>(March
3, 2011).</u>

[164]   Paul K. Jewett, *Man as Male and Female* (Grand Rapids: Wm.
B. Eerdmans Publishing Co., 1975), 142.

[165]   Ibid.

[166]   Letha Scanzoni and Nancy Hardesty, *All We're Meant to Be*
(Waco, TX: Word Books, 1974), 72.

[167]   "Men, Women and Biblical Equality," *Christians for Biblical
Equality*, CBE on the web at "Biblical Equality," 1989, www.
cbeinternational.org/?q=content/men-women-and-biblical-
equality (March 2, 2011).

[168]   David M. Scholer, "Feminist Hermeneutics And Evangelical
Biblical Interpretation" JETS 30/4 (December 1987), 408,
Journal of the Evangelical Theological Society, (Lynchburg,
VA: JETS, 1998, electronic edition by Galaxie Software, 408.

[169]   Ibid.

[170]   Stanley N. Gundry, "Response to Pinnock, Nicole and
Johnston, *Women, Authority and the Bible*," ed. Alvera
Michelsen (Downers Grove, Ill: InterVarsity Press, 1986), 59.

[171]   Ibid.

9 781662 893032